PARENTING ADHD KIDS REIMAGINED

HOW TO REGAIN YOUR CONFIDENCE AND CONTROL WHILE PARENTING A CHILD WITH ADHD

N. B. SHAW

CONTENTS

INTRODUCTION: WHY THIS BOOK?

Over the years, my research and experience helped me gain a new perspective on that wall that ADHD builds around a child. What we do not talk about enough is that it takes a family to pull down this wall. And at the forefront of this important mission are the parents.

Being the parent of a child with ADHD can be extremely challenging and isolating at times. The feeling of helplessness may loom large upon the parents as they try to figure out what exactly their child is struggling with. Is it the effects of ADHD? Is it their inability to express their needs? Or is it just how they respond? There is also constant pressure to create an environment conducive to the child's situation to help them be as successful as they want to be. *Parenting*

ADHD Kids ReImAgInEd will be your guide to dealing with ADHD through exploring the "only you know" (OYK) world of other parents raising their kids and formulating positive responses to the challenges that they face daily. Talking about the things that *only you know* or are willing to share is important, as this may ease the problems of many parents. Through this book, I give my readers a peek into the real-life situations of parents. But welcome to the new normal! This is how parents struggle with their children who have ADHD. Because you are the primary caregiver, you must confront your child's ADHD and the associated disadvantages with your child.

Consider this example: A parent shared how they had to call 20 different phone numbers just to find the right person offering behavior therapy to children with ADHD. This was their first "only you know" moment when they could not consult anyone. They had no connections with other parents who might have faced similar circumstances.

Why is it so hard to find the right person to help your child? Why is it so hard to find people you can relate to? Why does every road turn into a dead end? Who do you then turn to?

Even to this day, many believe that such symptoms are obvious. These are normal kid stuff. What they do not understand is that the intensity of each action and each thought that runs through a child with ADHD is ten times greater than normal kid stuff.

Teachers can get very upset about the child's behavior as well. I had another parent share with me how parent-teacher meetings turned into an absolute nightmare for them. It had only been a month and a half at this new school, and it was a new and difficult phase for the child. But instead of reaching out to the parent directly, the teacher chose to tell them how the child was a nuisance in class.

Telling the parent how their child is difficult to handle, does not focus at all, does not sit still, and constantly destroys the decorum of the classroom is not the path toward a solution. This is only passing the burden instead of sharing the responsibility. In this case, it induced guilt in the mind of the parent to the extent that she felt she had failed her child. She made constant efforts to make things work or bring at least a pinch of joy into their lives, but such harsh words only deflated her spirits. She used to wonder if anyone was listening to her at all.

This sense of hopelessness is common among parents engaged in taking care of their ADHD children. It can easily lead to burnout, resentment, anxiety, disappointment, desperation, and despondence.

This book, *Parenting ADHD Kids ReImAgInEd*, will assist you in locating the best professional to help you and your family. It brings to you, in simple words, the key elements to unlocking a potential and effective treatment plan. This book explains the benefits of creating a wholesome support system. Finally, it lists many practical solutions and tips for parents to regain their confidence and control by establishing a structured approach and strategy to better understand what causes ADHD in their child and how it affects them.

If you are one such parent who needs to be listened to and cared for, I would like to tell you that this book was written keeping you, your problems, and your experiences in mind.

THE ABCD OF ADHD

> *ADHD is not about knowing what to do but about doing what one knows.*

> — DR. RUSSELL BARKLEY

Kids weave stories in their heads all the time. Their mind space is like a factory of ideas. Whatever they absorb through their senses has a shade to add to the myriad of colors already at their disposal to paint the canvas of their minds. This stems from pure passion, curiosity, and creativity. This is also way before they learn what letters and words are.

But Darla had some very difficult times in her first few years because Andy was different from other kids. She could not tell the difference because Andy also happened to be Darla's firstborn, and no book on parenthood can prepare any mother for what is to come. Some kids have big emotions, and their behavior is a handful to deal with. Darla's story is similar. Initially, she felt her struggle was like every mother's until she spoke to her own mother and sister. Everyone noticed when Andy did not speak until the age of 3, but it was Darla's mother who raised an alarm when Darla told her about Andy. He did not turn over in his 4th month; he was not ready to crawl in his 8th month; and he did not walk until he was in his 14th month. "Some kids are slow," Darla would say to avoid piercing questions with a smile. But somewhere, she had begun questioning her own instincts.

A mother's heart is a garden of love. But humans also have certain behavioral limits. These do not limit love, but they do push us to seek answers to some pertinent questions. Darla was not doing this for the world. She was doing this for her child, just like many parents do. Matt, Darla's husband, made equal efforts. Reading more, knowing more, asking more questions, and consulting experts helped them reach the right answer. Andy was diagnosed with attention-deficit/hyperactivity disorder. But what was it, and how could it be dealt with?

A few months later, Darla and Matt found out that Matt's older brother, Jim, had similar issues when he was young. Kathy, Matt's mother, explained how Jim was shy at school, would find it difficult to follow multiple instructions, could not concentrate on studies, and could get very impatient at times. But they did not have a name for it then. Today, Jim is a senior journalist and has a lovely family. While this did reassure Darla that there was hope for things to get better in the future, more information made her question this even more. Is this a genetic issue? What if Andy has different problems? What if Andy does not do well in life? Jim had three younger siblings, which could have improved his situation, but Darla and Matt had no immediate plans for another child. How would that affect Andy in the long run?

We cannot get answers to all our questions about the future in the present. What we must understand is that in an ADHD situation, all our efforts in the present, no matter how small, will improve the chances of a better future. As mentioned before, every situation is unique, and they all need to be dealt with uniquely, but the efforts need to be uniform.

Are You Like Darla and Matt in Your Situation?

Disorder or not, the basic premise we need when dealing with a kid is that they absorb their surroundings. Whatever happens in their environment affects them directly. Your child will notice any lines of worry on your brow. Sometimes, in their low self-esteem or their hesitancy to make friends, kids ask for help. Their signs could be very different, just as their languages of love and understanding might be.

On the other hand, this behavior of their children can take a toll on the mental and physical health of the parents. Parents can be disconnected and may develop low self-esteem. The level of warmth, involvement, and love in the relationship with their child may go down. Work, relationships, and even responsibilities may all suffer from an unintentional attention deficit. Some parents may even feel defeated, deflated, and hopeless, with greater levels of anxiety and a slight loss of purpose.

Impatience, carelessness, and a lack of attention to detail can be upsetting, but we are all human. It is unfair to beat yourself up for human mistakes. Having a child who is suffering from ADHD can be tough on parents, but a deeper understanding of ADHD behavior and how to respond to such behavior may ease the situation for everyone involved.

ADHD AND THE RELATED NEGATIVE STIGMA

A disorder must never be seen as a defect. Sadly, in our society, most of us do not want to see beyond myths. Our investigations can help us differentiate between ADHD symptoms and other behavioral risks, but a lack of resources and a clear understanding succumb to societal notions. The real deficit is in our comprehension of the problem.

A child not following the ABCs is not a child who does not want to follow the alphabet. A wandering mind can make it difficult to focus. An adult may presume that the child is not following the instructions. What this adult does not know is that the mind of this child is a continuous theater. Different sounds, visuals, touches, voices, lights, and colors offer different distractions. These are the best friends and main vices a child with ADHD can have. They are best friends because these senses are their real school. Main vices because they are still gauging the limits and urgency of control, attention, and impulse. A child with ADHD does not have a slow brain. Their brains are as competent and as developed as any other child's brain. Nevertheless, the development of the brain is slower. In this theater, that is, the brain, there is less space given to the prefrontal cortex and basal ganglia. The role of the posterior inferior vermis, located in the cerebellum, is also small. These all are responsible for a child's focus and attention. But all these facts are unknown to the teacher teaching the ABCs to a class of 20 kids. For her, all her pupils are the same. A 3-year-old is like any 3-year-old who is shy and eager to go home. But there is more to shyness in kids with ADHD.

Here is a key difference: Shyness is about little eye contact and quiet responses. A shy kid may smile and like tasks like reading or coloring a picture. Appearing not to listen is not shyness. A kid with ADHD may not have an issue with eye contact. They will seemingly make efforts to get connected but fail at it. They may want to color a picture but will lose focus soon. Their impulse may lead them to do something very different, like spill water on the table or throw away the color book. Again, this is not being naughty or rebellious. An apparent shade of it, but not because they like being undisciplined or disinterested, but because behind their defiance lies a reason.

Their defiance stems from their inability to complete tasks on par with their peers. They try, but their minds could be too racy, giving them the impulse to run around the class. On this impulse, they can leave things behind. Forgetfulness is one of the major signs that develop early and can be tracked. They may remember the letters A, B, C, and D, but not that B comes before C. Additions can be easy, but subtractions could be very tough. This is where teachers and parents fail to understand the child. Such a child has a gifted mind like any other child their age. Their creativity knows no bounds. It is just that such brains need to be trained and treated a little more with care, planning, and affection.

The Fear of Labels

A lot of parents are scared of the labels that may get attached to their child who suffers from ADHD. The stigma around the disorder is real. Often, people do not realize how harmful it can be. It can damage a family. It can damage a life. It can greatly affect other lives that are related. Some parents are hesitant to lean on the side of diagnosis, prescription, and treatment. They fear that the process may inhibit their child's growth. Many also feel it is wrong to make kids medicine dependent at such a young age. Because of this fear, ADHD may go undiagnosed and untreated.

Fear of rejection, isolation, and social tags deepen this stigma. This may continue even as kids grow up and enter adolescence, and later, adulthood. These are teenagers and adults who may feel abandoned and misunderstood by their own parents. They would look for answers and halt in their tracks when they faced their parents. This is because of the disappointment they may feel in their parents, who, according to them, abandoned them in their problems.

This fear can also interfere with medicines, routines, and their effects. Elders' decisions about how to treat a child can have an effect on the child's life. It can have a negative impact if there is rejection. It can have a positive impact if there is support.

While ADHD may worsen mental health issues, not all ADHD patients have mental health issues. ADHD is not an illness. It should be seen as a learning disorder that can be dealt with rather than a mental health condition that requires a very different line of diagnosis and treatment.

Another reason that causes potential damage to any progress in this direction is the lack of right information. Many symptoms are confused with other behavioral issues. Symptoms also differ at different life stages. A toddler with ADHD behaves differently than a 10-year-old with ADHD. A teenager with ADHD would show different symptoms than an adult with ADHD.

Different Guidelines for Different Age Groups

There are very different guidelines for kids who are 4 to 6 years old than for kids who are older, 7 to 18 years old. For the younger group, behavioral management interventions are recommended. These could be in a class or in isolation. Methylphenidate is a prescription stimulant for kids at this age. For older children and adolescents, FDA-approved medication is recommended. Non-stimulant drugs like atomoxetine, guanfacine, clonidine, and viloxazine are approved. For patients who can tolerate stimulations, methylphenidate or amphetamine are considered. Parent training and behavior intervention classes are recommended for this group as well.

Parents need to support their kids during these guidelines and practices. They may seem challenging at first, but this line of treatment should not be misunderstood or mistrusted before it has been tried.

SOME FAMOUS PEOPLE WITH ADHD

Do not listen to the world if the world calls your child weird or different. Do not let others pull down your positive energy. Every child is gifted, and the only job parents have is to recognize this gift and keep reminding their child of how wonderful they are. The other job that parents have is to protect their child from anything that can snatch away this gift from them. And ADHD is not one of them. ADHD will not be a hurdle between your child and their goal. It is a disorder, meaning it is a slight disturbance, but it is not strong enough to be a damage. It is not a disease holding your child back. It is a collection of signs and symptoms that tell you about the difference in functioning of the brain. But it is neither a defect, nor a disruption. There are many popular examples around us to tell us that life can be meaningful, successful, and beautiful despite ADHD being part of one's struggles. Here are a few examples:

- **Emma Watson**: Most of us know her as the child actor who masterfully played the role of Hermione Granger in the Harry Potter series. Today, she is a brilliant speaker, a matured, well-read woman who is fearless when she shares her views, an Ivy League graduate, and a UN Goodwill Ambassador.
- **Michael Phelps**: As a kid, he struggled with schoolwork. He was diagnosed with the disorder at the age of 9. One of his teachers had

said to him that he would never amount to anything and would never be successful in life. Classic case of why we should not always believe our teacher? Or, maybe, why we should work hard to make sure negativity is not manifested. That is exactly what Phelps did and today, he has 23 gold medals of his total 28 Olympic medals. A record he could make when he found his way to focus and discipline. This was possible because he realized he could seek help when things seemed difficult.

- **Simone Biles**: She is probably the most popular gymnast of her times, if not one of all times. She was awarded the Presidential Medal of Freedom in 2022. She has medals from world championships and the Olympics. But her real fiat is making her audience sit at the edge of their seat as she plays out her body in the air. Biles was diagnosed with ADHD as a child and has used medication since then.
- **Adam Levine**: We all know him as the Maroon 5 lead singer. Being one of the coaches on The Voice gave him even greater recognition. We are talking about songwriter, rhythm guitarist, and rock star Adam Levine, who was diagnosed with ADHD in his childhood. He has previously shared his struggles with writing and recording

songs. When documenting ideas and making music became difficult, Levine realized he needed help. He was told that he still struggled with the disorder. His adult symptoms were quite different from his childhood symptoms. Today, he is very vocal about his persistent problems, continuously sheds stigmas around ADHD, and tries to remind fans that they are not alone in their battles.

- **Solange Knowles**: Solange was a gifted child. She started writing songs at the age of 9. In her elaborate and successful career, she gave America many dance hits. However, it took her a while to believe that she had ADHD. The first time, she rejected her doctor's diagnosis. She thought it was something her doctor had made up to charge her for the medicines. But she was diagnosed with ADHD again. This artist, singer, and songwriter advocates for the cause of ADHD, especially for Black children because they have a lower rate of this disorder's diagnosis. She is a shining example of creative success.

Some other famous people who are believed to have suffered from ADHD include Walt Disney, Albert Einstein, Leonardo da Vinci, Wolfgang Amadeus

Mozart, Agatha Christie, George Bernard Shaw, John Lennon, and Justin Timberlake.

No health disorder can inhibit excellence. These examples of famous people suffering from ADHD prove one thing: it is not an obstacle to a happy, fulfilled, and victorious life.

1

MAKING SENSE OF ADHD

A ttention-deficit/hyperactivity disorder is a chronic mental health disorder characterized by problems that involve focus, hyperactivity, and impulsiveness. It is often seen in little children, but the condition may persist into later years. It may cause difficulty in building social relationships, focusing on studies or work, lead to poor self-confidence, and cause severe mental health issues, including depression. Thanks to great therapists and medicines, ADHD is now less of a disaster and more of a disorder that can be lived with. We also saw examples of highly successful people who had come out of darkness to shine and make a mark in this world.

Around 3 to 5% of children suffer from ADHD. This makes it one of the most common conditions in kids.

Sadly, it is not always properly detected and diagnosed because the symptoms may vary from case to case, going very subtle in some cases. In most cases, it is diagnosed by the age of 7 or 8, but sometimes it goes undetected until adulthood. It is equally common in both boys and girls, but it manifests very differently. Because of its subtle nature, ADHD is diagnosed three times more often in boys than in girls. For example, two siblings with ADHD may show very different signs and symptoms. They may be diagnosed differently and at different stages, and they may respond very differently to the same treatment.

Sometimes, ADHD can seem like a lot. It can be a heavy burden. It can also be overwhelming. When this is combined with a few mental health conditions that may co-occur with ADHD, the symptoms are more severe and acute. But ADHD is still one of the most common neurodevelopmental disorders experienced by children across the world today. This is another reason why awareness around it is extremely pertinent. Despite its "pulling-back" effects, any human struggling with ADHD can be catapulted toward success and happiness.

ADHD IS NOT MENTAL ILLNESS

ADHD could be categorized as one of the many mental illnesses, but there are specific reasons why it should not be considered one:

- ADHD is a neurodevelopmental disorder.
- It can cause mental health issues like depression and anxiety, but it is not an illness in itself.
- The brain of an ADHD child could be developed more slowly than their peers, but nevertheless, it is a developed brain.
- As a deficit disorder, it is not a disease, albeit, a combination of symptoms, prominently making it an attention deficit disorder.
- An ADHD brain can have a plethora of benefits due to its "variable attention." Similarly, allergies and immunizations have no proven role in causing ADHD in children.

Poverty and chaos are also not the exact reasons for causing the disorder. A combination of effects, which may include poor nutrition or a lack of peace of mind, may increase the chances of the disorder, especially in certain groups of people, like hypersensitive mothers or mothers with an autoimmune disorder. ADHD is thought to be caused by a combination of factors.

However, two predominant factors remain: genetic and environmental. The third major factor is an imbalance in nutrition or any other kind of disturbance during key moments of the baby's brain's development.

- Brain injury due to falling or an accident may damage the brain.
- Exposure to heavy metals like lead, or poisons like arsenic in water, or other environmental hazards during pregnancy or infancy can directly affect the brain.
- Blood relatives, like parents or their siblings, with ADHD, any other neurodevelopmental disorder, or any other brain or central nervous system condition. Genes and heredity play a 25% chance of causing ADHD in a child.
- Prematurity is a high-risk factor.
- Smoking or drinking during pregnancy since alcohol and nicotine exposure may inhibit cell and organ development.
- Lack of nutrition during the fetus development or low birth weight of the child may lead to improper development of the brain and its parts.
- Improper blood circulation to the brain of the child.

- Extreme physical, mental, and emotional stress on the mother during pregnancy.
- Excessive maternal drug use or other drugs like sleeping pills during pregnancy.
- Brain function and anatomy: The structure of the brain varies from person to person. Brain development also depends upon brain usage. For example, lower levels of stimulation in parts of the brains that are responsible for attention and activity may cause its slower development. Some people are born with certain parts of the brain being smaller than other parts. Some studies have also directed toward a possible imbalance in neurotransmitter levels or chemical compositions in the brain. The gray and white matter is less in the brain of a child with ADHD than other children. The frontal lobes, caudate nucleus, and cerebellar vermis of ADHD brains are also affected.

ALL HAIL MICHAEL PHELPS

Michael Phelps has made every American proud with an astounding career where he bagged 82 medals from international swimming tournaments. He is considered the most successful Olympian with 28 medals, and a record high win for gold medals. Is this all to his achievements? Let us look at his struggles to understand why his achievements matter more than just the medals.

Born in Baltimore, Maryland, to Deborah Sue and Michael Fred Phelps, Michael Fred Phelps II was the youngest of three siblings. Swimming happened to him at the age of 7. By the age of 10, he had a national swimming record to his name in the "100-meter butterfly" event for his group. But not everything in life was positive. His parents divorced when he was 9 years old. Phelps later revealed that his separation from his father had greatly affected him. He was diagnosed with ADHD when he was in the sixth grade. In the initial stages, Phelps was prescribed the stimulant drug Ritalin. This controlled his hyperactive behavior and made him more focused and disciplined. In his autobiography, *No Limits*, Phelps shared that a reminder from the school nurse to take his medicine used to humiliate Phelps in front of his friends and classmates. He applied behavioral changes and used his mind to control his behavior and be able to focus more. This is where swimming proved to be a "boon" in his life, allowing him to be less dependent upon the "crutch" that his pills were. Swimming made him more disciplined and tapped his energy into something more productive. It made him less fidgety. As he grew up, he added records to his name. His doctor's continued support and his own renewed focus proved to be powerful weapons helping him approach his goal. Only the sky was the limit now.

The Teacher's Words

When Phelps was struggling with schoolwork and was not able to be attentive for a long span, his teacher told his mother that Phelps would not succeed at anything in life since he fails to focus on anything for too long. It is quite convincing to say that not only did Phelps prove his teacher wrong, but he also became the most successful and decorated swimmer of all time. He proved that medicines are not harmful. He proved that it is important for one to seek help whenever it is needed. He proved that ADHD brains are normal and sharp. He proved that ADHD is not an unsalvageable or hopeless situation. Above all, he proved that with strong conviction, the right guidance, behavioral alterations, persistence, and discipline, no goal is unachievable. Regular and rigorous practice channeled Phelps's mental and physical energy into something more ordered and relaxing. It changed his personality for the better. It also gave him a viable career option.

We cannot disregard his exceptional talent at swimming. We also cannot ignore the level of self-control, self-discipline, and self-commitment he had. But he also sets an example for every child suffering with ADHD, showing that their condition cannot be a road-block or defect in their life.

It is also a lesson for parents who are intimidated by diagnoses and prescription medicines. It is a light that must hold hope, and in this hope must lie the confidence parents have in their kids. The attitude of parents towards their kids has a very significant bearing on them. At the same time, therapy, behavior conditioning, medicines, diets, discipline, and physical activity must be given equal importance.

Phelps used his untapped energy to increase his swimming speed. There is untapped potential in each child that needs steering in the right direction.

2

SYMPTOMS

S ome of the symptoms of ADHD are visible early on. Some others are very subtle. The symptoms of attention-deficit/hyperactivity disorder (ADHD) can fall into two behavioral categories: the inability to be attentive and the issue of impulsiveness and hyperactivity. People may have both kinds of behavioral problems. In most cases, that is how the symptoms are. People may also have only one of the behavioral symptoms. Some people may find it hard to concentrate, but they may not be impulsive or hyperactive.

Lack of attention is a kind of ADHD called attention-deficit disorder (ADD). This may go unnoticed in many kids because it is not always very obvious.

SEE THE SYMPTOMS

ADHD is more easily detected in boys than girls because the lack of attentiveness precludes girls more than boys from leading a normal life. Because girls are more likely to develop inattentiveness, this symptom is not always diagnosed as an ADHD symptom. On the other hand, boys get diagnosed more often because of the disruptive (and more obvious) symptoms they may develop.

By the age of 5 or 6, most of the symptoms come to the fore. These symptoms, singly or in combination, are exhibited both publicly and privately. Let us look at these more closely.

Hyperactivity

Hyperactivity means being extremely active, sometimes even disruptively active. This harmless abnormal condition may occur due to disorders and behavioral changes but is primarily seen in children. It is also combined with impulsivity when a child suffers from ADHD. Impulsiveness would include speech and action without prior thinking or realization. Some signs may include the following:

- inability to be calm or quiet
- inability to sit still for some time
- finding it difficult to focus on a given task
- continuous talking
- excessively physically active
- unable to stand in a line or wait for their turn
- interrupting when others speak
- does not take no for an answer
- does not follow instructions
- does not understand the sense of wrong, danger or harm

Hyperactive children are constantly on the go. They can make others around them impatient, tired, and anxious. A **tip for parents** would be to engage the child in more physically demanding sports like swimming, tennis, gymnastics, and squash. Dancing and singing can also make such kids feel purposeful. Their impatience, energy, and impulse can be tapped and trained. These, combined with behavioral therapy and discipline, can hone the unseen and hidden skills of the child. A younger age is great to instill values of hard work, honesty, fairness, discipline, perseverance, and respect.

Inattentiveness

Inattentiveness means a lack of attention. Kids with ADHD often find it difficult to concentrate. Their focus is not laser sharp, and they can be constantly distracted. Some of the indicators are as follows:

- short attention span
- continuously distracted in either thoughts, or by talking, or scribbling, or simply not listening
- easily losing things like pencils, erasers, sharpeners
- easily forgetful and often uninterested
- making mistakes and not learning from them. For example, writing any letter or word while doing schoolwork
- time and energy consuming tasks like coloring a book, sitting in a classroom, reading a book, or following any instructions may seem tedious
- constantly shifting from one activity to another
- could sometimes be disrespectful, rude, and disobedient to appear uninterested when they are struggling deep within to focus
- may find it difficult to play puzzles, tie shoelaces, or organize things

These problems could pose significant struggles in the life of a child. It may be burdensome to make friends, be confident, focus at school, or be disciplined.

This is the child who you may feel is a daydreamer. This child is mostly quiet and lost in thought. A **tip for parents** would be to engage with such a child through the medium of arts, music, colors, and visuals. This is a great way to unleash their creative potential and get a peek into their thoughts.

Other Signs

A few other conditions that could be related are:

- antisocial behavior like fighting, quarreling, harming other children or animals, stealing, and lying
- anxiety and nervousness causing dizziness, sweating, and palpitation
- negative and disruptive behavior toward elders, teachers, neighbors, and relatives
- irregular sleeping patterns
- fatigue
- epilepsy
- depression
- showing no clear interest in any activity
- issues with learning and remembering

- difficulty in physical coordination

How Do You Differentiate ADHD Kids From Other Kids?

At some point in their childhood, every kid is prone to impulsiveness, hyperactivity, and inattentiveness. It is very natural for little kids to be distracted or have short attention spans. Older children and adolescents may also find it difficult to concentrate on a task for too long. Their level of focus usually depends on their level of interest. Younger kids are also little storehouses of energy. They are potentially moving powerhouses. Most of them are hyperactive, loud, chaotic, and not tired even after their parents are. Just because these children are more energetic and active than their peers and siblings, they cannot be tagged as having ADHD. Some kids could be shy at school but have friends at the local park. Some other kids may have problems with schoolwork or understanding numbers or letters. They may have trouble following instructions. This could be because of how the brain processes, stores, and uses the information. These are signs of dyslexia and are different from ADHD. Some toddlers may have few facial expressions. They may seem shy, but they could also be very talkative. These symptoms could be those of a child suffering from Asperger's syndrome. As these kids grow up, their symptoms become clearer. AS can be diagnosed by doctors in kids as young as 18 months old.

If your child shows signs of ADHD, it is recommended that you see your doctor or pediatrician. If necessary, they may ask you to consult a specialist. You may also refer to a psychologist or a pediatric neurologist for more information and a deeper diagnosis. Medical examinations and evaluations, along with medication and therapy, may help improve the signs of ADHD and keep other complications in check. It could make things easier for your child.

Other Complications or Coexisting Conditions

ADHD may not cause other neurodevelopmental disorders or psychological issues. However, certain conditions may coexist in children along with ADHD.

- Anxiety may include overwhelmingness, worries, nervousness, panic attacks, or obsessive-compulsive disorders (OCD).
- Conduct disorder that may include antisocial, disruptive, or destructive behavior.
- Mood disorders which may include depressive episodes, bipolar disorders, and angry, irritated, frustrated, and emotional phases.
- Learning and communicative disabilities.

- Substance use disorders.
- Autism spectrum disorder that affects a person's perception of and socialization with others.
- Tourette syndrome which causes sudden and repeated twitches, sounds, or movements. These are called tics.

DIAGNOSIS

To evolve strategies to counter ADHD, one has to understand the causes and symptoms of the disorder. Every child is special. The debilitating issues associated with ADHD can be severe and can make life very difficult for a child if not timely diagnosed and treated.

SIR RICHARD BRANSON AND HIS SECRETS

The British billionaire, entrepreneur, and business mogul, Sir Richard Branson, founded the Virgin Group in the 1970s. Even in his personal life, he has succeeded in maintaining excellent relationships with family, friends, and co-workers, had a great run at his humanitarian endeavors, and was brilliant at sustaining great physical and mental health. Whatever preconceived notions we may have of people having ADHD, Sir Richard Branson's life and accomplishments can prove them all wrong. Let us get a glimpse of his life secrets:

Have a Morning Routine

For Branson, a morning routine is where healthy habits can be inculcated. To be successful, there are certain things you need to add to your morning before the day begins. For Richard it is

- waking up early in the morning
- doing his favorite exercises
- having a healthy breakfast

Exercise Everyday

Physical and mental exercises are extremely helpful for people with ADHD. Exercise is beneficial in many ways, but the best is that it brings you closer to your goals. Richard says. "You have to be fit. If you are fit, you can achieve anything." Some ADHDers find it difficult to follow one exercise routine. Richard says there are two ways to counter this:

- Firstly, make sure the exercise you do is fun for you. If you do not find it interesting, you would lack the motivation to do it at all. For him, it is playing tennis everyday with someone who is younger and fitter than him. This keeps the sport challenging and fun. He also goes kitesurfing.

- Secondly, mark your challenge. You can find something interesting if you have something to achieve through it. A goal or a challenge is a reminder that may help you focus better and have fun. For example, a marathon is a great challenge. In his words, "You don't need to get boringly fit; you need balance in life."

Avoid Sugar

Sugar is bad for all kinds of bodies. Excessive sugar is worse. While there is no evidence that sugar causes ADHD, sugar intake may worsen the symptoms of ADHD like hyperactivity and affect the level of insulin secretion by the pancreas. Branson says to do everything to avoid sugar.

Get Out of Your Comfort Zone

It is extremely important to get out of your comfort zone. To gain more experiences and achieve more from life, one must push beyond boundaries. Comfort zones have limitations, and it is beyond these limits that life has more to offer.

Accept Yourself as You Are

Acceptance is the key to a healthy and happy life. When you accept yourself the way you are, you respect your boundaries better. You know what your realistic goals are, and you plan your moves better. These plans are very important for facing reality. If they do not work, one does not blame themselves. According to Branson, one should not be embarrassed by their failures. Failures must be learned from to inspire new beginnings.

This is crucial because ADHDers can blame and criticize themselves for what the world sees as "flaws." This negativity has the power to bog down the power of positivity. For not meeting the deadlines, for not being able to be as organized as their peers, for not reaching their goals at a given time, and even for a late arrival at a place, there are some incidents where ADHDers go above and beyond to be hard on themselves. This may cause a continuous loop of negative emotions. This can also remind them of what others have said.

Keeping yourself motivated is the biggest challenge for a person with ADHD. This is even tougher for little kids. A **tip for parents** would be to be a gentle reminder to their kids that acceptance is a very big gift. It is comforting to know oneself and then maneuver one's way toward one's aim. Pushing boundaries is only viable when one assesses these boundaries correctly. Criticism only leads to exhaustion and demotivation.

Intuition Is the Best Guide

Intuition is a part of acceptance. Pushing boundaries can be a great challenge but listening to intuition is mindful and rational. That is the fine line between pushing your boundaries and exercising restraint. Listening to your intuition is necessary because it best judges the situation. Richard recalls a time when he had to make a jump from a 100-story Vegas building. His intuition was against it, but he jumped under pressure. Branson says one needs to know when to "pull the plug." He knew it, but he did not pull it. As a result, he jumped and injured himself.

See the Positives

We need to see the good around us. Surely there would be a lot of negatives but focusing on the positives would help us focus on ourselves. It enables us to see the positive in the people around us. Branson stresses the point that there is always something special about everyone. We have to see ourselves and others with kindness and without prejudice. With this positive attitude, we may be able to better tackle the tasks as well.

A **tip for parents** would be to cultivate healthy habits and emotions in their kids with ADHD. Sharing the achievements of ADHD-positive people may also prove highly instrumental. Such kids require more attention, care, love, and encouragement. Their timelines could sometimes be delayed; they may be slow to complete their schoolwork; they may not get all the instructions correctly on the first attempt, but on other days, they may be very focused and active. These energies, if tapped and channeled in the right direction, can build up a person's character.

3

SIX KEY CHALLENGE AREAS OF PARENTING AN ADHD KID

P arents lose confidence when their child does. A child may look engaged or happy momentarily, but their condition may upset parents since their vision is now blocked by a disorder that manifests in their lives each day but whose very existence is the cause of its illusion.

ADHD is not always very prominent in its presence. It can be marked in the behavior of some kids and very subtle in the behavior of other kids. Why it happens is also a complicated question since there could be many factors and their combinations leading to it.

In this chapter, we will look into the six key challenge areas of parenting an ADHD child. While there are many challenges on this path, I have combined the roadblocks into six broad categories. These include organization issues, logistics issues, relationship issues, school issues, home issues, and emotional issues.

This chapter explores how these factors impact parents' confidence and control while raising a child with ADHD.

Your understanding of these problems and their root causes will also help you understand and develop the solutions. Regain your confidence; it's in your hands. As parents, your last bet should be on regaining it, if not for your own sake, then for your child's sake.

MONDAY MONSTER

It was a relaxing weekend for Darla. She felt refreshed. Matt was away for two weeks on a work trip, and she was at home with Andy. As opposed to her initial fears, the time she spent with Andy was very comforting. The two watched films together. She would cook his favorite meals. During the evening, when Andy went away to play with his friends, Darla got some time for herself. She even played some piano, surprisingly well considering she had not touched the instrument in more than two years.

As always, Monday morning came knocking on the door with a newspaper. Darla was making breakfast when Andy came to the kitchen in his night suit. To her shock, he had not gotten ready yet when it was already so late for school. Was this the same child who was so sweet and obedient the past week and a half? He was ready even on the weekend, and now, when he had to get ready to go to school, he was sitting in front of the TV. When I inquired, he answered nothing. He did not even bother looking up. After calling out his name several times, when Darla went to switch off the TV, he shouted no. With pleading and prowling, Darla finally got the little man ready, only to find his shoes and backpack missing. Repeated questions had just one answer: "I don't know. I don't remember."

She slumped down on the floor in defeat, anxiety, and dizziness. Six-year-old Andy was close, but not close enough to see what his mother was going through.

This is the story of a lot of parents. When one has a child with ADHD, one does not know what to expect. Finding it difficult to get your child out of bed and out the door for school as well? This is the story of a lot of parents. When one has a child with ADHD, one does not know what to expect. It could be a myriad of experiences, most of which are unexpected, sour, and sometimes even bitter. Ensuring that your child is safe at all times compromises parents' sanity. This is the reason parents are required to focus on the challenge areas that seem to overpower them in some form, from time to time. Let's have a look at each one of them.

ORGANIZATION ISSUES

As the name suggests, it is linked to the basic challenge area of organization. Parents of Kids with ADHD struggle with all kinds of organization. This is tougher for kids and a primary challenge area for their parents. You could be at your wit's end trying to make sense of what is happening in life or at home. On top of it, your stress makes it worse.

Let us look at a few ways you can keep your home and child organized:

- Small beginnings: You cannot master tidiness and organization at home if you have a child with ADHD. You would want to have a perfect house, but chances are that everything is upside down. A **tip for parents** is to not try everything at once. Focus on smaller tasks and one task at a time. You may take longer than usual, but you will reach your goal. As you proceed, you will feel more accomplished. Trying to manage everything at once will not help you. You will not only lose interest but also not achieve any of your goals.

- Declutter: If you have little kids, that too one with ADHD, chances are that your house will be a complete mess. This is not because such kids cannot be trained. They can be, but it would take some time and patience, and they are not the sole reason why you should declutter. You should declutter to detach and feel more organized. The less you keep, the more memories you create. It is a great activity to be engaged in to feel productive.

- Accept that perfection is a myth: No matter how much you try and how good you are at organizing things, there will always be that one task that remains incomplete. Perfection is unrealistic and unachievable. Work hard and trust your instincts but do not crush yourself with overload, especially when dealing with a kid with ADHD.

- Assign tasks to yourself: Try to manage a few tasks yourself. If you are a stay-at-home parent, there is a limit to the work that you can get done because there are unlimited chores in the house. If you are working from home, good luck with that because you will have to work doubly hard. This does not mean you do double the number of chores. This means you need to distribute the tasks well according to the days of the week, and also to other members of the household. Try to accept that there is a limit to your capacity.

- Note down everything: Make a list and follow it. Your tasks should be planned, and your list must be well-thought-out. Spare some time for flexibility because there is always a chance for one unseen, unpredictable moment that can bring you some extra work. A **tip for parents** would be to keep a whiteboard or a challenge for kids with ADHD. The sooner they learn to be organized, the better for them.

- Work on your focus: Puzzles, meditation, and exercise sharpen the focus. As a parent, you would need more focus to manage both the house and the child with ADHD.

LOGISTIC ISSUES

Logistics mostly include your executive functions surrounding your child's life. These may be their transportation, their activities, their homework, doctor's appointments, therapy schedules, and preparing meals for them.

This is tracking their daily life with codependence. It is easier to face this challenge by following a plan. To not be overwhelmed or stressed, do the following:

- prepare the coming week's timetable in advance by using a planner
- have designated space for articles, like important files, books, snacks, and stationery to avoid confusion and last-minute panic
- use a lot of visual schedules for the child, for example, stickers, drawings, chart papers, magnets, and highlighter pens
- inform beforehand if you would be late from work to pick them up from school or practice
- involve them in activities like grocery shopping
- keep them updated regarding their therapy sessions
- talk to their teachers about tests and surprise tests and try to be ahead of them by introducing the lessons
- always have an extra bag in your car with their clothes, toys, snacks, comb, and other essentials
- introduce them to the concept of time and schedule with mild discipline

RELATIONSHIP ISSUES

Parenting kids with ADHD can change the household dynamics. It can change the relationship between partners or parents. It can bring about differences between siblings in how they are treated and brought up. It may also change the family's relationship with friends and relatives.

It will not always be easy to put the child's needs above the family's and doing that can leave irreparable cracks in the walls holding these familial bonds together.

A simple way to do this is by keeping things uncomplicated. Fair and regular talk between family members must establish the rule that no one person is burdened with all the major work. Each family member must get some time away from the overwhelmingness of the household.

Self-prioritization in the form of self-care is extremely necessary for parents. Keeping hobbies and interests alive, taking walks, joining an interesting language class, building a support system from scratch, taking care of mental health, and reading more about other things of interest will bring a person closer to themselves. It is very important to detach shame from ADHD parenting. This can be done when you understand that you have the "gift" of parenting that others do not. Firstly, they will never go through your struggles, and so they do not have the right to dictate whether your methods are right or wrong. You need to distance yourself from anyone who berates you or your parenting. Secondly, remember that you do not have to prove anything to anyone. You do not have to conform to norms that do not apply to your home. Thirdly, accept the mess that your family could be in most of the time, but also accept the beauty of the mess. Do not compare your family with other families. Acceptance comes with full recognition on your part that this is how your family is and that it is normal in every aspect. Lastly, never hesitate to ask for professional help.

For siblings, this may be a completely different scenario. They may feel guilty that they are well. Because their siblings with the neurodevelopmental condition may require more attention, the other kids may be hesitant to ask for help, advice, or any attention from their parents. They may behave as if everything is fine, but in reality, they may be anxious, depressed, frustrated, embarrassed, and looking for attention outside the home (this sign should be a concern). These kids would need their family's full support to navigate their relationship with their siblings as well as the outside world.

Finally, kids with ADHD find it very hard to socialize. This may not be so prominent when they are little, but as they grow up, how they differ from their peers gets more attention. The difficulty in making friends is mainly due to:

- low confidence
- shyness
- inconsistency at any task
- weak attention span
- hyperactivity
- being easily bored
- less awareness
- frequent interruptions
- not very strong sense of bonding

For this, make sure you have the right therapy for your child. The atmosphere at home and at school should be tender, helpful, and kind.

SCHOOL AND HOME ISSUES

Because of their difficulty paying attention at school, some rules are always missed by kids with ADHD. They may have a problem understanding the concept, which may lead to poor grades. A teacher-parent joint effort may help the child improve their focus. Apart from the therapy lessons, there are many exercises to increase the attention span. When it comes to behavior, your child must be clear about the behavior that is expected of them.

Such kids may be asked to slow down. They may be given more attention, prompts, time, and incentives to be engaged in the task. Their careless mistakes can be discussed with parents later.

Because these kids demand more time and attention from their parents, they also demand the same investment when they are away from home. This is not possible in school or anywhere else. This also makes the attention-deficit child very attention-dependent and attention-loving. For your efforts to be fruitful, you need to make sure that your rules are as much appreciated as your love.

EMOTIONAL ISSUES

Seeing the child struggle and have recurrent troubles can be very difficult for some parents. Their only attempt would be to suppress their feelings and engage themselves in daily chores and attending to their child. This suppression of anger, sadness, nervousness, and helplessness is not healthy. Part of nurturing relationships is also having a sense of balance. Many parents are facing similar struggles as you. There are support groups, both online and offline, to help parents like you. Bits of advice, suggestions, sharing, and caring can relieve a lot of burden from your shoulders. The experiences of people who have gone through a similar ordeal are as helpful as books, magazine articles, and podcasts. To cope with your feelings, you may consider journaling, therapy, or talking to friends and family. Do not ignore channels of communication for the sake of commitment to your household and family members. A self-care routine is a part of self-help, just as maintaining healthy boundaries is a part of self-respect.

Controlling Emotions: A Guide for Parents

The sea is calm as long as there is a hurricane. We would love to blame the winds and the oceans for it, but as it proceeds toward our coast, we have to protect our home. Many couples fight because they feel the sea of emotions emerging from ADHD must not have a room in their home. It is a defense mechanism; we all want peace to prevail. But it is the chaos that reaches before the hurricane that is more worrisome, as it has the power to destroy harmony like no other catastrophe.

You cannot change your child's ADHD. You can change your attitude around them. I am not asking you to become immune to the criticisms and struggles that are about to come your way. But there are ways to stop emotional expressions from turning into explosions.

I will not present a parallel narrative that all is well in such homes. Everyone around a hyperactive child tends to get super emotional at least once a day. Mostly, it is the other family members who are more in need of help and therapy. One major area where parents get stuck is emotional regulation.

Emotional regulation stems from emotional bonding. This bonding is the one a person has to have with themselves. In easier words: your emotions are your responsibilities.

Since we need to teach this to a child gradually and very patiently, we can practice this on ourselves and recover from our own emotional complexities.

There is no quick fix as to how you are feeling, and there are no guarantees that you will feel any better any time soon. With your child's delay in brain development (again, it is a disorder, not a defect), it may take them a good 2–4 years to encapsulate what others around them are feeling because of them. In the meantime, it is you who has to take care of everything and yourself. Here are a few ways you can do it better than you think:

- By observing time: Quite literally. Look at the clock on the wall and try to have a sense of time in the context of your present situation. Watch your emotions in an intimate affair with time and you will calm down. It may take minutes or even hours, but when you are watchful, you spare others from a melodramatic meltdown. I say this more as a concern because meltdowns are exhausting. You can still be expressive without bottling up your emotions, but with a child full of energy, scope, and rage, your meltdown has little centerstage. You are your own audience in this spectacle. Emotional outbursts are very difficult, but it is more difficult to manage them in the aftermath. Put things in a better perspective and seek help whenever possible before your emotions get the best of you.

- Investigate the past: Find solutions to the present problems in the past. Recall your "best self" as a parent. Your problems today might be very different from back then but that does not make the past troubles trivial. Leave little reminders of encouragement and love for yourself at your work desk, in the kitchen, and in your bedroom, and read these tiny pieces of affirmation every day. Pay close attention to how they make you feel and then have a brief conversation with yourself without any prejudices. Confide in a close friend or a family member if you need some extra help and support.

- Avoid being harsh: If you are angry, try to have the least interaction with your child. Do not say anything that you later regret. Children may not be attentive, but they are sensitive, and they remember. What you want to communicate must not come from a place of mental and emotional trauma or defeat. You cannot compromise your calm during heated moments, or all your efforts will go down the drain.

- Reflect: It is very important to take some time and see why you are feeling the way you are. You must investigate where your emotions are stemming from. The root cause of your distress is very often not your child and your complaints but something else. As a parent, your job is to make sure you protect your child from your own unfair exasperation.

- Have a calm conversation later: Make sure everyone is at the table to have a calm conversation. You can internally gauge your level of stress, tiredness, anger, weakness, and annoyance. Not all family members will be on the same page, but at some point, everyone must sit together and try to hold each other's hand, because, at the end of the day, your family is one unit.

- Show kindness: Be kind not just to those around you but to yourself as well. Sometimes your kids may attack you with very mean, unfair, strange, unsettling, and scary accusations. Feeling hurt, angry, broken, or helpless is quite normal. Except for, you do have help around you only if you want to look and seek. Be kind to yourself in the sense that does not push yourself beyond your limit. It is also nice to have a self-care regimen as part of self-care because you would need it from time to time.

SIMONE BILES, THE SHINING STAR

Simone Biles is a known name across the world. She is also one of those star athletes whose medical records were hacked and then released publicly. According to the World Anti-Doping Agency, she was approved to take a prohibited drug without naming it.

Biles soon released her statement to end the barrage of questions that were unleashed on her character, hard work, and honesty. She reassured everyone that she followed the protocol and shared information about her ADHD condition. She also mentioned that she has been taking these medicines since she was a young kid. As a believer in clean sports, she spoke about her trust in fair play and its critical importance in any championship. She said she was not ashamed of her ADHD condition or the fact that she has to depend on medication.

This is probably the biggest takeaway from this story. ADHD is normal; it is common, and its existence should be acceptable. People shy away from such discussions because they either do not want to reveal what they see as a *weakness,* or they do not want to give someone else the power to know something personal about them. It is a matter of choice, but people who want to talk about it must witness a safe world around them as well. There are a lot of notions attached to ADHD, but at the end of the day, it is just a condition and a common disorder.

4

THE 4 PHASES OF PARENTING GOALS

Parents want to feel confident about what they are doing. They may follow a lot of instructions and technicalities, but it is the learning from their own experience and the experiences of other parents they interact with that makes the most sense.

To better navigate this disorder, parents must first be mentally prepared; and second, shed the stigmas surrounding ADHD. The third step is to have a structured approach to understanding what their child is going through. This chapter is about different phases of parenting goals. Just like the child, parents also go through different stages, determining their approach and chances at survival and success.

The first phase is about motivating the child. The second is to model organization in their own life and the life of their child. The third phase calls for support —mental, physical, and emotional. The final phase is about cheerleading for their child and championing their cause.

These goals are necessary for parents to make sure they are not completely absorbed in their child's issue but also have a solid plan of action to not be overwhelmed or disappointed from time to time. This plan of action keeps reminding them of their ultimate goal, which is to help their child and not surrender to ADHD or adjust to it for life.

PHASE 1: MOTIVATING YOUR CHILD AND DIRECTING THEIR WORK

A child with ADHD does not compete with their peers. Their competition is with themselves. Their competition comes with days that make everything more difficult for them. Their competitor lies within them who pulls them back from being more attentive and alert. It makes even the most mundane things, like making a list or taking down notes difficult. It makes the kid believe that they must have a grave problem that makes them seem foolish and slow.

Motivation is what keeps a child or adolescent with ADHD going. It pulls them out of bed, makes them work hard to be better versions of themselves, tests their patience, and rewards them in the end. As long as the strategies you apply work, all is well and good. If they do not, there are other ways to keep your child motivated.

The first way to do it is by changing the environment. The same environment can make things mundane. To make sure your child is not bored in the same setting, you can make changes to their schedules, lessons, and the place of learning. The key to dealing with ADHD is not to change the child but to tweak other factors. This does not mean abrupt, sudden changes that may induce anxiety but lively, present-day atmospheres that give them options and challenge their minds, talents, and skills.

Research has shown that participative and creative tasks allow disruptive behavior to soften. The "what" and "how" of the curriculum are equally important to keep the child motivated. Only rewards and good grades do not drive kids toward improvement. It is the strategies that foster continuous motivation:

- make sure there is a structure to your lesson
- an environment where the child feels comfortable
- simple instructions
- mental stimulation at each step with something new to learn
- clear rules and limitations
- pragmatic expectations
- well-spaced breaks
- physical space for movement
- uncomplicated assignments
- alternative methods of assessment
- rewards for good behavior

How to Approach

To attain the above, you need to follow a few simple steps. Kids with ADHD are not immune to insults and insensitivity. They are not ignorant, and they do sense the perceptions people may have about them. As they grow up, their restlessness may combine with aloofness and indifference. They may lose motivation to socialize, work harder, or even go to therapy. Let's look at the ways you can approach them as a parent:

Allow a respectful space: Depression, anxiety, helplessness, and impulse may have signs, but you do not have to be too close to your child to help them. You can do that even from an approachable and accessible distance. Being present is not the same as being overbearing. Your child also sees that their progress is not linear, and they may be falling behind. This can tear anyone's confidence apart. Make sure your reminders are not adding to their troubles.

Try collaboration: Do not expect short-term gains. Choose a path that has a long-term plan. I am not saying that plans do not fail. They do. But do not lose the bet before placing it because you are too afraid to try. Your child is worth the risk and effort. You only have to make a sensible plan that combines their present hard work with a future goal.

Gaining from goals: Many parents have told me during my research that goals are best achieved when incorporated with interests. Again, for someone with ADHD, there can be a wide range of interests and activities to choose from, but the aim should be more than just a short-term interest. It should be linked to a long-term plan. These goals must have a specific meaning in your child's life. Take theater, for example. Learning lines can be tough for some. Stage fright could be distressing. But the passion for acting may surpass it all. The goals are achievable only when they are realistic, but factors like timing and resources greatly impact this achievement.

No fake rewards: There should be no place for fake promises, smiles, or rewards. Every praise must come from the heart, every smile, unforced, and every promise, genuine. Try to keep interactions simple and warm. Your child may grow up to be distant, but they still deserve to know they have a safe home to return to. If you over assess or underestimate their qualities and achievements, they will learn to do the same to themselves. Something like seeing how much they have worked on a particular assignment or how proud you are of them because their performance has improved can be very uplifting. Refrain from using statements like "you deserve it more than others," "you are exceptional," or the generic "you're so amazing." Apart from this, you must:

- let your child know of your realistic expectations from them
- provide regular feedback
- respond to their calls of help
- be patient

PHASE 2: MODEL ORGANIZATION IN LIFE

Organizing begins with acceptance. A child with ADHD must embrace their condition. They cannot deal with it if they segregate it from their being. Taking ownership of their disorder is taking charge of it. This may happen in the following ways:

- Teach kids to recognize their symptoms as the first step to managing them.
- Managing techniques must be healthy coping mechanisms and no forced interventions.
- Organizing schedules with therapists and doctors.
- If medication is chosen, a regular ritual must be in place. One cannot miss them or have them as per convenience.
- Relaxing techniques, physical exercises, and mental and emotional state management are necessary to this endeavor to organize life.
- Healthy behaviors do not come only from therapists. They come from daily, persistent, and genuine efforts.
- Children follow their parents. The first step to organizing the child's life involves organizing your own life by eliminating chaos, confusion, complications, and clumsiness.

- Organizing life also entails time management. Help kids prepare their own schedule when they are old enough. This teaches them self-reliance and gives them little room to complain.

With self-reliance comes self-reflection, and with self-reflection comes self-help. In my experience, when your child is so close to recognizing themselves, they also begin to recognize their symptoms.

They will learn ways in behavior therapy to calm these triggers, but they will pass the test when they apply this knowledge in real-life situations. Organizing their lives helps them organize their brains. This helps in the better fulfillment of the major tasks at hand. There is no avoiding work now. Kids can be taught to journal and devote words to their emotions. For example, if they need to study for a history test, they can begin the simpler way. They can count the number of pages and check the important sections. Next, they can make a schedule and mark the important lines. Be it an individual or group setting, I would say it is the child's call. Let them create a checklist and check the listed options one by one.

Organizing memory is compartmentalizing it, but some minds are used to multitasking. Such organizing also maintains healthy conversations. A positive and calming response from parents would also help kids be better motivated for the future.

PHASE 3: SUPPORT THE OWNERSHIP

With the conversations I have had with parents and teenagers, I have realized one thing: owning the situation is making peace with it. When you make peace with your being, you are not disregarding the disadvantages; you are regarding the advantages. It does not mean defeat; it means acceptance. It is empowering to accept your situation, but it is even more empowering to now take control of it because you are no longer in denial. A **tip for parents** would be to try motivating, emotionally stimulating, and supportive statements like, "I know you have ADHD, but you are a lot more than your condition," and "I know it is very hard sometimes, but the examples of some of the most brilliant minds, creative and successful people prove that it cannot stop you from being awesome" or "Your condition is a part of you, but there is no issue with your brain. It just works a little differently from others."

Transferring ownership is not just transferring responsibility. It also entails transferring power. This happens in a series of steps:

- making your child or adolescent with ADHD believe that they can manage their own symptoms
- helping them learn this management
- letting them makes mistakes
- allowing them to learn from these mistakes
- giving them space when they need it
- winning their confidence through care and not overprotection
- can withstand transition
- will learn with time
- need to be patient at all steps

Medicine Management

As long as your child is with you, it is wise to administer medicine and dosage for them under the doctor's guidance. Middle and high schoolers may be given this responsibility, but that passes on to their shoulders gradually. Their pill intake must be under supervision. Other experts like doctors, therapists, and teachers must also be kept in the loop during such a change. There are a few things that your adolescent must know before they are handed over the prescription medicine:

Medicines must be taken only according to the dosage prescribed. More pills do not give better or quicker results. I have gone through various studies that show that adolescents are more prone to taking medicines under pressure. This may be before an exam or during the week. Some even tend to miss them before an event, while others may take an extra dose if they feel anxious or need to focus more on a certain task. This is risky, as it does not improve the situation but worsens the symptoms. Any changes in dosage must be done with the doctor's consultation. One must have medicine according to their plan if they are away because these cannot be brought simply without a doctor's recommendation. These medicines can also not be combined with alcohol or illegal drugs.

On the other hand, medicines have to be kept safe and away from others. Any other person cannot take them only because they feel they have similar symptoms. There are no mental stimulation medicines to better focus on studies. A violation of these rules is illegal and can be dangerous.

PHASE 4: CHEERLEADING AND CHAMPIONING YOUR CHILD'S CAUSE

To champion your child's cause, you have to be their advocate both at home and school. This begins with a deeper understanding of your child. It is not fair to place your expectations on your child's shoulders. If you see your child through a lens of prejudice, so will the world. Besides, you cannot see your child through the tinted lens of presumptions.

You have to be their voice and speak up for them in a world that does not accommodate "the different ones." This requires a lot of strength. When they grow up and learn to fight their own battles, they will still need your emotional support and words of encouragement. We can credit ADHD here because it is this journey of life that strengthens the bond between parents and their children.

Here are a few simple ways to be a cheerleader for your child:

- **Ask the right questions**: It is very important to ask your child all the right questions. This is your effort to communicate better. Some kids with ADHD may be very talkative. Some others may not speak at all. In either case, communication channels open ways for your child to redeem their confidence. Simple questions about how their day went, who is their favorite teacher, the subject that they do not like, or watching their favorite show with them will be a great way to break the ice.
- **Recognize your child's behavior**: Your child's teacher may tell you about their behavior at

school. You can track the progress of your child and compare it with their behavior at home. Some kids do a sum correctly at home and do not do it at all or do it wrong at school. This is because of their confidence and trust issues. How the student-teacher relationship pans out also determines your child's behavior at school. You need to be in touch with the teacher and discuss the child's strengths and weaknesses.

- **Asking for help**: This is a significant part of cheerleading for your child. It is very important to make sure that their mental health is not compromised in any situation. Having a perspective about someone's child is very different from having a comprehensive inquiry and evaluation of their behavior. At what stage, how, and from whom you get help for your child determines their academic excellence, emotional stability, cognitive presence, and social relationships.

- **Plan according to your child's mood**: I encourage healthy communication between parents and their children because it has the power to maintain harmony at home. Not all plans that adults make may go according to your child's moods, but some must consider their needs. Just as the education plan you choose for them depends on specific factors like teachers, experts, evaluation standards, and past results, personal plans must consider mental health, social coordination and company, performance at school, emotional expressiveness, and physical activeness.

A FATHER RECALLS HIS DAUGHTER'S STORY OF SUCCESS WITH ADHD

This is the story of a father and his daughter. For privacy reasons, we will call him John. His younger daughter, Kerryn, was different from his older daughter, despite the physical resemblance. She would cry more, not sleep well at night, and despite her brilliance and intelligence, she would not respond to affection or hugs. It was difficult for her to form meaningful relationships. She was either too offensive or painfully shy. The older she grew, the more disorganized her life became. Her good performance in sports could not hide her rude conduct with others. Her behavior was unpredictable and sometimes even terrifying. As parents, John and his wife were extremely worried, anxious, and helpless. With an IQ of 140, Kerryn could not win a single scholarship in her last year of primary school. Over the years, her performance deteriorated, and this bright girl descended from the top level to the other faction in her class. When she mingled with individuals with unhealthy and unsafe behavior, the parents had to put their foot down.

I would ask the parents reading this book, "What would you do in such a situation?" It was hard for them to control an unruly teenager, but they took the fortunate decision of moving her to a different school. She made new friends who were supportive, welcoming, and productive.

When John was approached by one of Kerryn's friends' fathers, he realized he faced a similar situation with his eldest daughter. This is where I want to highlight the role of community and friends when dealing with a kid with ADHD. It was a new dawn for John. Their situations were each other's reflections. Up until now, he did not consider ADHD seriously, but the more he read and researched, the more he realized what they were missing. With input from pediatricians and psychiatrists and results from neurological tests, it was proven that Kerryn had attention-deficit disorder (ADD) without hyperactivity.

Today, Kerryn is one of the top ten students in her class. She takes her medicines on and off with the doctor's consultation. She has enrolled herself in a tough university course, and she likes to be focused, quick, and productive on the sports field.

John is proud of his daughter. Her room is organized just like his life. But he feels he was one of the fortunate ones. Had it not been their decision to move her to a better school in a healthier company, he would not have crossed paths with another man who was kind enough to help. But there are many Kerryns and many Johns out there who are unaware and in need of help.

5

HOW TO HELP YOUR CHILD COPE WITH ADHD

J ust as kids who have ADHD are different from kids who do not have ADHD, two kids with ADHD may have distinct dissimilarities in behavior too. I would urge people not to label their children in this regard because a child with ADHD may have more in common with a child who does not have ADHD than another one with the disorder. This happens because there are many layers and nuances to this disorder. There is no one-size-fits-all solution to ADHD, which is why we employ different strategies to build a child's confidence and deal with their behavior.

To the world, these behavioral symptoms may look like tantrums. But it is the lack of self-esteem that causes the child to act in bizarre ways. Andy's condition was worrying his mother, Darla, each day. He had symptoms of impulsivity, difficulty learning, an inability to focus, hyperactivity, and limitless energy, but it was when he started shrinking inward that Darla was scared. "He was a very talkative child, but he would not talk. He was unable to maintain friendships. Everything that was happening in his life was too much and making him tired," Darla would explain. "I did not know what to do; he was only 7."

ADHD AND SELF-ESTEEM OF KIDS AND ADOLESCENTS

ADHD can be overwhelming. Detention, suspension, low grades, and poor social behavior can disrupt the life of a little child. They may feel different from their peers, who are making progress, can focus on school-work, and make friends easily. On the other hand, when kids with ADHD see their parents and teachers lose patience, they start believing that "something must be wrong with them." A **tip for parents** would be to step back and analyze the entire scenario from a third person's perspective. Criticization, dismissive feedback, and correction may frustrate and demoralize a child. This could pull down the child's self-esteem and lead to depression. Watch your language. You can say, "I really appreciate your hard work in keeping things orga-nized," instead of "Why are you so messy?"

Parents must recognize the success of their children. They should know what they are dealing with through the help of research, therapy, and guidance sessions. These are a few simple ways to help your child gain confidence:

- Give genuine compliments focusing on the child's strengths.
- Remind your child how much they matter to you. Show your trust in the child. All the success stories of ADHD portray a very healthy relationship between the kids and the parents. It is all about the affection and warmth you give.
- Do not overlook other children because some cases of ADHD come with guilt and the need to clear animosity and sibling rivalry. You have to make sure your home is balanced and peaceful.
- Discuss their interests and explore future career paths together. It could be art, music, sports, or even comedy. In my experience, children aged 8 and above are capable of stating what they like and what they do not. Some like to be the class clown, what is the harm in that?
- Work hard on your child's weak areas. Darla had to make sure reading and writing were as much fun for Andy as math was. This was a

long road where she mixed his reading sessions with other interesting books that tickled his curiosity and imagination. for language and comprehension, he hired a tutor.

- Stop making unfair comparisons. Avoid putting any pressure on them because you have unrealistic expectations.
- Be in touch with the therapist, pediatrician, or specialist you are consulting for your child.
- Do not overlook it as "just a phase."
- Be the model that you want your child to follow. You cannot lecture kids on good behavior unless you show them what "good" is and what they should be like when they grow up.
- Share your emotions with your child without burdening them with the negatives. you can share sweet and fun memories to have them invested in the brighter side of life despite the struggles that they face.
- Talk to your doctor about medicines to control anxiety if therapy alone does not work.
- Tell your child that their life and passion are much bigger than just their condition.

Dealing With ADHD Behavior

Always remember that perfection is a myth. Every child is unique. You cannot keep all kids with ADHD in one group. There are a few simple strategies that can help you as a parent be more careful when dealing with a child with ADHD:

- Do not break the routine, especially the timings of homework, play, meals, and sleep. Some exceptions on some days are not a big issue. But a healthy routine is a groundbreaking ritual.
- Make sure your instructions are simple, brief, and clear. All tasks must also be divided into clear and small steps with friendly reminders.
- Try to give healthy reactions as much as possible. Yes, a lot of times you would get impatient, frustrated, angry, and impulsive. But remember that that is not the model you want to set for your child.
- Remember that your feedback matters the most to them.

PARENTS' PERSPECTIVE: WENDI'S PERSONAL STORY

ADHD is the name for a group of different, hard-to-explain feelings that a child may have. This name gives people a different perspective on a child than the terms lazy, disinterested, slow, and menace. It categorizes their behavior as a neurodevelopmental disorder for deeper investigation. This can be daunting for parents sometimes. Some may feel their child is not normal, and others may not believe in the diagnosis at all. Some parents may have felt that their child is not perfect, despite appearing that way. Some others are embarrassed to go in public only to deal with their child's impatience and impulses.

Wendi's story is similar. She saw her son, Drew, finding simple schoolwork hard. He was unable to understand concepts his peers easily could. He would hit his friends despite being told not to. In his T-ball league sessions, a 6-year-old Drew could be found picking dandelions on the margins of the field. When he got enrolled in soccer classes, he could be found playing with a drinking fountain in the outfield. Apart from his Lego masterpieces, he hardly found anything else interesting. A lot was going on with Drew, but sadly, Wendi took it as a challenge to make sure her efforts made him "normal."

This continued even after he was diagnosed with ADHD at seven. Wendi finally decided to sign him up for Boy Scouts and become the troop leader.

Wendi found that weekend hikes were seemingly improving Drew's state. His interest could have been piqued by anthills and dirt on the way, while Wendi carried both their backpacks, but Drew was finally showing signs of improvement.

Their next adventure was a 30-mile canoe trip down the Colorado River. But the water did not excite Drew. The moths around the night lantern had his interest more than the daytime activity of paddling. Wendi's first day was long, exhausting, cold, and disappointing. She fell behind all the other canoes because Drew did not help paddle. The next day, despite paddling with double her strength, they were left behind by other canoes in the river.

For the first time in her life, Wendi wished she had a son like others—a son who could hit a home run, kick a goal, and paddle a canoe. She soon, however, realized how wrong that was. In front of her was her beautiful son, gazing into the water to spot a fish. He was so special that he did not need a race or reward to smile; just a butterfly sitting on top of his shoe could do that. He did not want to be the fastest. He wanted to slow down, look around, be curious, explore, and be happy.

6

BUILDING A ROUTINE

When parenting a child with ADHD, struggles are inevitable. This may be the right time to consider routines. A routine in place should be such that it benefits both the parent and the child. This set schedule may help provide structure and stability in the lives of both kids and parents.

Impulse, aggression, a poor sense of judgment, and poor executive functioning skills cripple the child, their freedom, and their imagination. A routine is an attempt to organize daily activities in the hope that it will bring some order, organization, and discipline to unruly life. It does not necessarily mean a strict regimen. Routines can be friendly, too.

If you look up ADHD on the internet, you will find no recipe for a routine. There is no fixed routine for all kids with ADHD. Just as no two kids with ADHD are the same, no two routines can be the same. It also varies from family to family. It also depends on their experience and range of exposure to treatment techniques. ADHD also affects each child differently. Some may be full of energy during the day and fast asleep at night. Others could be very shy and quiet during the day but may wreak havoc in the house as soon as the clock strikes seven in the evening. To make matters worse, the bonds that each family shares and the lessons that they learn along the way are very different.

WHY DO WE NEED A ROUTINE?

There is a lot of flexibility about what kind of ADHD routine must be chosen. As someone who has done thorough research in this field, I would like to say that it is up to the parents, as primary caregivers, to determine the routine according to their child's patterns. For older children and adolescents, a routine must be set according to their needs, temperaments, schedules, and activities. But leaving some room for flexibility in the routine is as important as sticking to it with honesty.

Here are a few reasons why we need routines for ADHDers and how they can help:

- **Schedule, structure, and order in life**: An organized setup is, to some degree, a predictable setup. This structure is created by bringing order and management to life. Take time management as an example. When you and your child know that 6 p.m. is dinner time, it is predictable, it brings order to life, and one can manage the later events accordingly. When there is no fixed dinner time, the entire evening gets wasted. Similarly, a rough plan for college allows hard work and gives some liberty to that hard work. There is a goal, and there is a period set to achieve that goal. It is an entirely different thing if one does not achieve it but working under a schedule prepares students for college life with a much broader course structure. A **tip for parents** would be to introduce a routine early in a child's life. It not only manages time but also helps to regulate emotions.

- **Lesser conflicts**: There is more harmony in the family because there are fewer arguments regarding tasks, events, and timings. This gives a chance for the members to have better relations. With minimal skirmishes and less approving behavior, there is an improved change noticed in the lives of the people of the household. A set routine helps to cope with anxiety, stress, and change. Better interpersonal relationships and healthier habits also add to the overall health of all the family members.

- **Helps regulate activities**: A routine provides for a more structured life, which means a more empowered life. There is a positive sense of control which means apart from regulating activity and behavior, one may save time to accomplish more tasks. When one does more work in a stipulated amount of time, it has a better effect on mental health. Positive regulation of activities may help an individual feel more productive.

- **Structures habits into the routine**: With better focus comes better dedication, and a greater sense of responsibility. Kids learn to do their chores on their own. Some learn to cook; others do their own laundry. Older kids and adolescents inculcate a more serious outlook toward studies, grades, and potential career choices. There is a sense of independence and self-reliance. Many also begin to take their medicine routine more seriously.

- **Brings more discipline**: With more skills and habits, the value of scheduled, structured, and organized work is understood better. Once one starts enjoying their routine, discipline comes naturally. Self-discipline is a skill one imbibes on the way to becoming a healthier, happier, and more fruitful individual.

- **Involves the entire family**: A family routine does not single out the kids. It is something that all the members of the family follow. It does not apply only to children or adolescents, which means they feel part of the whole structure on a deeper level. There is a fixed time for homework, showers, meals, or television. A routine may not make life easier, but it makes it more manageable. Keeping the clothes and books in an organized way to find them easily the next day is also a part of the routine.

- **Key to success**: Organized and disciplined behavior is key to a successful life. A routine may help tame the hyperactive side by conserving energy and the power of creativity and imagination and using it elsewhere such as in dancing, gymnastics, swimming, or horseback riding.

YOUR ROUTE TO ROUTINE

A proper routine can minimize ADHD symptoms over time for a variety of reasons. For starters, it relaxes the child with ADHD. Secondly, it makes the child used to a well-established set of rules. Thirdly, the child may feel safe following the routine with their family. Fourthly, the child may devote their energy to more productive tasks. And finally, it adds better habits to their life, like sleeping early, eating timely meals, and reading more, which may help the child focus better and have more confidence.

A few tips may help create a routine that works for all:

- Involve the child at each step to avoid confusions. It is extremely important to involve the child while creating a routine. It gives your child a say, empowers them, and there are more chances the rules would be followed.
- The rules must be uncomplicated, crisp, and crystal-clear.
- A lot of accomplishments in a little time is impossible. A step-by-step process is the one that is recommended.
- Rules must be kept flexible. Sometimes there may be calls for adjustments. The child must understand the concept of flexibility, and small

changes and transitions should prepare them for times when rules and routines do not fully apply. As long as a general timeline for things is being followed at home, sticking to routines should be fairly simple and easy (sometimes even fun).

Make Consistency Your Companion

A successful routine is the result of clear instructions and consistent effort. Make sure you have your child's full attention by turning off the television and dismantling all other distractions. When you speak with your child, there must be eye contact. Try to be gentle when imposing rules. You can place your hand on your child's shoulder to gain their trust. Do not confuse your child with a lot of instructions and rules. There should be one instruction at a time.

Many people ask me why I recommend no distractions for your child. For a child's brain, which is already everywhere, unhealthy distractions can pull them to a new low. Yes, television may keep your child engaged for a while, while you are busy with the chores, running your engine of efficiency, but unhealthy engagements can reduce their efficiency.

It does take a little more effort to engage with your child directly and sit with them as they read a book or color a diagram, but you cannot expect your 9-year-old to clean their room with your one-time instruction. You are bound to be disappointed. It's better to build a routine here.

For example, every Saturday morning, your child will be task to clean the bookshelf. Every evening, they will help you set the dinner table. These little engagements make your child responsible while keeping them on your radar. The rules that you set must be clear: make your bed. For some kids, taking instructions could be hard. In such a case, you can ask your child to repeat what they just heard.

Make sure you praise your child's every effort, even if they are bound to the routine. Every time your child helps you with a chore, a "thank you" will not hurt. If your child is tired, give them a break, but do not over-look any misbehavior, no matter how mild.

Above all, make sure that your child understand that their actions have consequences; some will be met with praise and rewards, while others may be met with a stern stare or a mild punishment.

LIFE WITH A KID WHO HAS ADHD: A SNEAK PEAK

No parent with a "normal" child can ever fully realize the problems that parents of kids with ADHD face. Every single minute is intense. If I have to put it simply, these parents must be doubly attentive to their inattentive children, meaning they have to share the burden of attentiveness.

Nothing holds their curiosity for too long. Exhausting is a small word. Instructing a child whose body wanders more than their mind is like supervising, instructing, and negotiating at different levels, sometimes simultaneously. Sometimes the power of chocolates and ice creams also fails to woo them. You may feel they will sit down for their favorite meal and then be up again after only two bites of food. No, they are not done with their food. They will come back to it, but there is some fire burning more passionately than their hunger right now.

Today, they may enjoy the swing. Tomorrow, they will only pick flowers and play in the dirt. No amount of advice from pediatricians, psychiatrists, and psychologists builds a force strong enough to encounter this little child's intensity, curiosity, and distraction.

I am not trying to dissuade anyone from making use of these services because they will save you energy, time, and life, in short, but the concept of a peaceful and normal day is absent from the lives of such parents. Incidents that can be very difficult and events that may leave parents embarrassed are not isolated; they spring up every now and then. But the isolation that these parents feel is more persistent.

I asked a few of them if it was frustrating. "Sometimes," some would say with a weak smile. Truth be told, these parents love and value their children no less. Darla was not frustrated because her son Andy was different. She was angry and frustrated because she felt different every day, yet still defeated and a little more destroyed. It is not always because parents have high expectations. It is mostly because no parent can see their child in pain, confusion, failure, or loneliness and be at a loss for words to explain what they are feeling.

Yes, sometimes parents may feel they had an easier life and an easier child, but would they wish for another child to replace this one? Never. The constant battle with, for, and around your child is tough. But parents need to find the courage to get help before it leads to a full-blown nervous breakdown.

Trust me and my wealth of experience; parents, you will require a lot less energy investment in therapy than you do every day. The impacts and counter-impacts of what happens in the house affect the family dynamics because it does not remain a normally functioning family anymore. A lot of other stuff comes home with your child's school bag. Even holidays and festivities are not normal. In my opinion, during an argument, just as you are going to lose your patience, wait and hold that tongue. Think about a child you made with love and the mindless clutter and added-on pressures that have led to this mess.

It is never the child, nor your relationship with your spouse or other kids. They are trying as much, and they care as much. Their ways to show affection, attention, and appreciation may be difficult. But this is not the end, nor is it a sinkhole that you as a parent cannot come out of. This is where you end your quarrel and let peace thrive, because peace leads to better decisions, be they about the family, the kids, the food, or the therapy.

7

CREATING A SUPPORT SYSTEM

Kids with ADHD have uniquely wired brains. Hence, creating a support system for them becomes a prime necessity. Such kids demand more time and attention from parents when compared with other kids. ADHD can bring a pivotal change to one's routine and how they view relationships. If you are a parent facing this kind of situation, there must have been times when you have felt alone and lost. Loneliness is another strong emotion that remains with such parents because they find no one to share their problems with. Parents may also feel misunderstood at times. It is important to remember that there are many people who may understand your problem and support you and your family. You only have to reach out.

WHY DO WE NEED A SUPPORT SYSTEM?

A support system for kids with ADHD is essential. For parents with a child with ADHD, it is an indispensable service. It may act as a system of emotional support. Parents may be able to connect with other parents, therapists, and other medical professionals who can share their knowledge and experiences because they all have something in common. These groups are equipped with the right kind of advice, resources, information on treatment, and the latest research. These groups not only act as a forum to discuss common problems and experiences and share advice, but they also provide a stable structure, instilling confidence in both parents and their kids.

What Are the Benefits of a Support Group for the Parents?

Support groups could be a way to create massive positive change when parents ReImAgInE their way around dealing with a child with ADHD. These could be the constant companions that many parents need but are not so vocal about.

- They allow you to share programs, stories, learnings, unique experiences, references, sources of information, and even battles of frustration and disappointment.

- It's a great place to learn more about social events like training workshops, bonding exercises, services, school initiatives, and other benefits. Because of this, coping with challenges gets a lot easier for parents.

- These are places to build long-lasting friendships not just for parents but also for their kids. A mutual advantage for parents who can share tips on childcare since caring for an ADHD kid is distinct from caring for other kids. This is path breaking since parents may be exhausted, frustrated, and stressed with the methods they follow in isolation.

- They may also share childcare responsibilities to give each other relaxation breaks. This is because they understand the kids' needs well. This is a great way for parents to gain trust and confidence in themselves and others too.

- Siblings and other family members can also attend these support groups for activities and events and strengthen support. There is also a way to find and connect to other parents, families, and support groups on the internet. Although, face-to-face interaction could be more beneficial to build a strong and valuable sense of support and community diminishing the factors causing social seclusion.

- There could be other local groups, NGOs, and health service providers that may come to assist and have a positive influence on parents and families. In short, they can be your trusted source for referrals.
- They help parents gain a practical perspective on things. Such an influence leaves a positive influence on the child too.
- The support through these support groups is not restricted to one area of life like the ADHD of your child. It could be extended to other dimensions like mental, emotional, and physical health, personal growth, interpersonal relationships, peace and happiness, and a better understanding of life.
- Every ADHD challenge is unique. Apart from the common behavioral challenges, such support groups offer suggestions and instructions regarding treatment and strategies associated with specific challenges unique to a case.

Benefits of Support System on Kids

- It is difficult for kids with ADHD to make friends. With a support group to engage with, your child may feel understood, reassured, and connected with other kids going through a similar ordeal. It may provide a safe environment.

- Kids exhibit improved performance in academics and sports after attending such support group sessions. Some even became more participative in extra-curricular activities like dance, theater, music, and arts.

- There was a marked reduction in behavioral issues. Many kids were now less impulsive and hyperactive, and more patient and stable.

- There was an improvement in the social and emotional status of the child. The supportive network proved to be beneficial for the child.

- Some kids may have very subtle to very mute symptoms that may make not only the diagnosis but treatment also problematic. In such cases, support systems can make a determining impact.

HOW TO CREATE AN ADHD-PARENT SUPPORT GROUP?

When we say ADHD, we do not see emotions and struggles. We only see the name of a disorder. Most people would not even know about the struggles the kids suffering from ADHD have to go through on a daily basis. Those who do know about it would not consider the struggles that the parents have to go through to make sure their child is all right even while battling with something known, yet, unknown. This is where conversations need to flow and the best way to have them is by organizing them with people with similar struggles. I have been told by parents how disappointed they feel when they know about some-thing similar happening in another region, but no scope of such an event in the place where they reside. One article, one conversation, one program can steer some-one's life on a better path. When parents feel they can help themselves is truly when they can help their kids as well. These sessions are not just about comfort and rewards, they are also about fun and connections.

Choose Your Support System

Feeling lonely in your battle with ADHD is normal and natural. But it is not easy or obligatory. These feelings can be abandoned with the right approach. Fear, sadness, doubt, and dissatisfaction must be balanced by feelings of satisfaction, joy, courage, self-assurance, and commitment.

The notions and pessimism around therapy and medication do not allow a holistic development of the child. On the other hand, the isolation may make every family feel unwelcome. This is where networking comes in handy. Today, many adults believe that had they and their families been supported better during their growing-up years, many of their present-day obstacles would have been diminished.

Determining Help

A lot of times, parents start blaming themselves for their child's disorder. I once met a man who said that their child was probably suffering as a result of the difficult pregnancy months his wife had to endure. Maybe. Maybe a mother's mental health has a pivotal role to play in the mental development of a child, but who is to prove this, and how do we detach guilt from parents? This is where we need to determine the help one may need. Apart from therapy, friends, families, colleagues, and neighbors can play a major role in supporting parents, especially during the late childhood and early adolescent years. This support in the form of respite, affection, warmth, care, and attention may go a long way in cheering up both parents and their children.

Define Your Team

Trusted friends, family members, extended families, therapists, and behavior coaches may not care for the child as well as a parent can, but sometimes they stand like a force to support you as you raise your child. A kind neighbor whose kid is willing to play with your kid, a family member who is ready to babysit your child, or a colleague who may help you feel positive about your job and is ready to step up to help you professionally are all part of your dream team. Talk to more people, share your problems, do not see it as a "sympathy card," choose people who choose you, and above all, include people who will not fail you as your team members.

Look For Local Support

Local support groups close to your home, workplace, or kid's school could be a great help. People here would care more because they would also relate more to your journey. A simple search on the internet for ADHD support groups in your area would give you some more clarity. It can give you a list of such groups that are functional around your location. It can also give you links to NGOs and other national and regional sources and meet-ups.

Include Teachers

Your kid's teacher could be a very good daily observer for the improvement in your child's conduct. They are a vital part of your child's life. This may include the child's classroom teachers, behavior and speech therapists, counselors, music or sports teachers, librarians, and even guidance coaches. By making them part of your team and talking to them often, you can make sure that your child gets support and care that they might not get otherwise.

Consider Training Programs

Training programs can coach you about the exact needs of your child. For example, in America, the National Center for Parent Information and Resources provides local centers in each state. It is directly funded by the U.S. Department of Education. They could be a good starting point for researching support networks and connecting with other families in the area.

Prioritize Community

Your community may have a unique identity and culture. They may also have different activities and programs to keep the families in a close-knit circle. There could be events for kids of different ages, from art competitions to poetry writing contests to singing contests. Some may have swimming or chess competitions. Similarly, there could be dance programs or pep talks for teenagers and recipe-sharing get-togethers for adults. You could meet people from your neighborhood and other neighborhoods. You could even meet people from the same church or the local library. These people may have a lot to offer when it comes to helpful resources for you and your child.

Choose Family Members

Who do you turn to when your child is sick? Who do you choose when you need a piece of advice or immediate help? Research has shown that family members spending quality time together leads to a direct connection, a healthy ritual, better mental and physical health, a channel for communication, more chances of showing affection, healthy eating habits, reinforcement of positive behavior patterns, a better routine, and a safe and much-needed distancing from technology. A cousin's birthday, an outing with grandparents, a family wedding, and a festive celebration all add more vibrant colors to the canvas of childhood. These also have productive effects on the lives of the parents.

Help Yourself

As a parent, your priority must be to help yourself before you decide to help your child. Being a parent does not mean that you are responsible only for care-giving. You are equally responsible for receiving care. Your health conditions must not be pushed beyond your limits. Some parents may have passed down ADHD to their children genetically. But this could also mean that their own condition was left undiagnosed. In other cases, some parents may be equally vulnerable to other mental health issues like anxiety, eating disorders, neurodevelopmental disorders, depression, loneliness, or rejection. This means parents go through a lot, often in silence and isolation. Parents must make sure that they ask for the right help at the right time for themselves too.

Step-By-Step Process

During my research, I have come across many heartbreaking stories. But I have also come across heartwarming and hopeful stories. People are gradually accepting that there is indeed light at the end of the tunnel. People are less scared to talk about the condition of their kids now. More people come forward and join social support groups now. Parents have also realized that they cannot exist in a vacuum. No problem is solved in isolation. Here are a few ways we can achieve social support by forming groups.

- You may form the group alone, or with other people. Two or more families may come together for a group as well.
- A favorable location is more inviting for people. Generally, a coffee shop close to a park, a church, any local community hall, a place close to a health center where people may go to weekly therapies, or any place suggested by an NGO is comfortable, familiar, and free of cost.
- Usually, once or twice a month is preferred by most parents. Friday evenings or Saturday mornings could be more ideal than a weekday.
- Flyers, posters, and pamphlets at common and popular public places, as well as newspaper or local advertisements, can be a few ways to spread the word.
- Some people may feel comfortable speaking in the beginning. Some others may choose to speak at the end. The standard procedure may include a brief (15–20 minute) introductory session and then move on to sharing the problems and experiences of parents. A person

could note down or record the important points made during the discussion.

- Collective brainstorming to find ideas and solutions is a great way to look for answers to common problems. Some topics could be pre-chosen, and some could be evolved. Parents can also decide the topic for the upcoming session to have plentiful time for preparation.
- Fun activities can also be planned with kids to keep them engaged.
- Fee can be a matter of choice. A nominal fee may keep the advertisement line open and also a way to send out the invitation to any relevant speakers. However, the fee must be nominal and not discourage parents from joining the group. It should be affordable for all.
- Parents must be reminded about the time, theme, and place of these scheduled meetings. Not all can make a mental or physical note of the same. Responsibilities for the same must be equally distributed.
- No few members must feel crushed under the burden of arrangement and organization. This would be a sustainable way to maintain consistency.

THE JOURNEY OF HOWIE MANDEL

When actor, comedian, game-show host, and mental health activist Howie Mandel was growing up in the 1960s, there was no name for his disorder. He had the symptoms forever, but he got the name for them only in the last decade. As a child, his home was as difficult a place as his school. Things were so tough for him that he could not even complete his high school diploma. Even today, in every conversation that he has with his family, his loved ones remind him to pay more attention. But love was never an issue in his life. He says he never felt unloved by his parents. He has been married for 30 years, and while his wife and kids have admitted that living with him can be a little difficult sometimes, it is love that has sustained him over the years.

His rash decision to reveal on a talk show that he had OCD and ADHD nearly broke him, but since then, many people have approached him and shared their own experiences. It was not just comforting and relatable; he also realized the need for people to talk more about their suffering since most people suffer in isolation. His conditions have helped him live a fulfilled life. Today, he owes much of his success to his comedy, which reflects both his ADHD and OCD. However, he finds it difficult to sit still and read or write a script.

What he is coping with owes its identity to four letters, but what he is coping with is something only a very small number of people would truly know.

8

UNDERSTANDING THE IMPACT OF ADHD ON YOU AND YOUR FAMILY

A DHD does not just alter personalities; it alters an individual's personal life. It does not matter if your child is young or an adolescent; their ADHD condition will have a bearing on the quality of their lives. From how you show affection to how you control anger, you would observe a slight shift in your model of parenting. This realization becomes more acute as you learn about your child's disorder. Your focus may change, as would your emotional, mental, and physical capacities. For some parents, their tolerance level may expand; for others, there might be a considerable shrinkage.

A family is not untouched by what their child suffers from. Their adjustments (and sometimes sacrifices) are ways to cope with the situation. This can be taxing for all the members, especially the parents.

THE EFFECTS OF ADHD ON KIDS' PARENTS

- It can be extremely exhausting. Parents do not often talk about this aspect because they do not want to carry the guilt of prioritizing themselves or showing their fatigue face to their child. In reality, parenting a kid with ADHD is extremely energy-draining. Keeping up with the child's energy level and mood swings is unpredictable and tiring.
- It does not always give the desired results and parents may not feel fulfilled at the end of the day. At the same time, it can be extremely stressful to see your child all over the place.
- Your efforts as a parent may not always protect them from vulnerability. They could be overly sensitive about an issue. But they may also feel nothing at some points. These on-and-off extreme switches can be very confusing for the parents.
- Further, the segregation of the child may create a gap in the relationship. Behavioral disturbances like isolation, low self-esteem, and

depression and developmental disturbances like slowness, confusion, impulses, and failures are hard for parents to watch. The feeling of helplessness is the most crushing.

- Educating self and keeping up with the information may look like a never-ending battle. Sometimes, logical reasoning does not give the right answer. I once had one parent tell me that it's a bit of all - mind, heart, skills, behavior, and physical strength, when dealing with a child with ADHD. We cannot undermine any of these factors.

- Parents are also under a financial heavyweight. Not all therapies are free. Not all skill-building classes, medications, special education, or behavior management courses are accessible. This situation can also cause productivity loss of family members who are caretaking.

- There are times when parents fight among themselves regarding chores and decision-making. There is no doubt that responsibilities on both parents increase manifold when the child has additional necessities and demands. Parents need to be on the same page to avoid conflicts. Different approaches and styles of parenting may lead to arguments. If unchecked, these may cause strain in the relationship and even resentment.

- On the other hand, the stressful environment of the home may worsen the condition of the child. The responsibility comes down on the shoulders of the parents to find the end to this never-ending loop.

- If such a kid has one or more siblings, chances are that they may be left attention deprived. This can affect their performance and grades too. This neglect happens very subtly, but it alters the way the family functions.

- Stress may also make parents vulnerable to a range of minor and major health problems. Anxiety, restlessness, palpitation, overprotectiveness, aggression, insomnia, and nervousness in parents are common fallouts. Parents also keep worrying about their child's future. These trials can turn even headstrong parents into powerless and tense beings. How a child is treated in public, by their peers, classmates, neighbors, and family members affects the behavior of parents as well.

- Rigorous parental monitoring is as dangerous as reduced monitoring. A lot of times, parents fail to find the balance between the two. Any imbalance may lead to a disturbed parent-child equation and sabotage it for life.

- Finding parents who have a non-ADHD child but understand you and your child's situation is difficult. People tend to stick to their groups, with little possibility of including a newcomer.

Over-expectations may hurt. As a parent, you cannot expect your child to stop watching television immediately after your command. They will not sit still for too long, and they will not make progress at schoolwork in one day. ADHD would not let them. It requires continuous support and a lot of self-restraint to improve your child's life.

It can be difficult to find life's true meaning and values because your life will not be like most parents'. But every parent needs to find joy and peace in their situation. It is a choice we make, and it is the values that we create that we ultimately pass down to the child. From habits to behavior, thoughts to action, and conscience to kindness, our children learn from what they see in us.

FACING AND MENDING THE IMPACTS

When I say *reimagine*, I want to reimagine and manifest ways through which parents can gain control over their children's lives. By control, I mean affirmations and hopes that play out to create a harmonious environment in the house, leading to the holistic development of the child. ADHD is a parenting battle, and it can be won if the parenting approach is right.

Not all that we see with ADHD is gloomy. Not all those who are discouraged and face difficulties ultimately fail in life. There are strategies to cope with the impacts of ADHD. There are parenting techniques that can be applied to twist a situation in our favor. Organization, curiosity, eagerness, and willingness to learn can change the life of every child and adolescent who is facing ADHD as an obstacle. But let us look at the way's parents can mitigate the impacts that befall them.

- **Dial the number**: Do not stop yourself from asking for help or social support. Help is just a phone call away. Parenting is easier, more fun, wholesome, and more effective when parents are healthy and have ready help for themselves whenever they need it. Having friends, family, neighbors, and colleagues on your team, childcare, economic aid or minimum wage, and emotional support through therapy and connection with other parents make the job less isolating. In case you live away from friends and family, local units of parenting cooperatives, online help, parenting communities, guidance classes, and therapies can be extremely helpful.

- **More involvement**: Following the improvement trajectory and communicating regularly with the trainers and therapists is an indirect route for involvement. Direct involvement with your child, in their routine and curriculum, their habits and hobbies, and in their interests and likes makes a strong parent-child bond. More warmth, affection, hugs, and kisses are ways to tell the child that they can reach out to their parents at any time.

- **Investigate your stress clues and causes**: Watch out for symptoms and signs of stress. Does it hurt your back, head, or any other body part? Do you feel exhausted and anxious? How much time do you devote to your hobbies and happiness? Take out time for something meaningful and relaxing like painting, music, reading a book, or exercising.

- **Counting**: Considering how overwhelming the situation can be any last moment or unexpected changes may ruin the entire day. But one must try not to give away this power to the situation. Mindfulness through meditation and deep breathing exercises can immediately calm down a parent's anger. Tell yourself to "breathe in and breathe out". Other times counting backward from 10 is also very helpful to help you relax and give more clarity.

- **Warmth instead of worries**: We have already discussed how kids sense stress. Forgetfulness, clumsiness, short temperament, and apathy can soon be imbibed by kids. This does not mean that parents need to put a mask on all the time. Parents must take small breaks to recharge themselves. This is where the role of family, therapists, and community comes into the picture.

- **Communicate more**: Help your kids with schoolwork. If they are on medication, check the time and dosage regularly. Talk the kids through next week's schedule to prepare them in advance. They may throw last-moment mood swings. But just as you gradually learn to keep your overwhelmingness under control, you can teach it's breathing exercises and mindfulness too. This would help them in the future too.

- **Make the child responsible**: Your job is not over by placing food in front of your child. But it also includes making a bond over food. It is also valid to closely listen to what kids have to contribute to the conversations. The confidence that the child gains from this makes them believe that they are being heard and have a place in the home to be themselves. They need to know that their feelings and thoughts are accepted.

- **Get enough sleep**: This is a very crucial factor in keeping you healthy and stable. Sleep-deprived people are more stressed, and prone to cardiovascular problems, mental health issues, obesity, diabetes, breathing issues, and chronic pain in the body. Sleep hours and patterns may affect your decision-making capabilities, memory, focus, alertness, and judgment.

- **Embrace your emotions**: You need to accept that ADHD cannot be cured or eliminated. But that does not mean that your efforts are purposeless. Do not suppress your positive or negative emotions. Do not be scared of failing but do not be scared of dreaming either. It is common to worry for your child but do not brush these worries under the carpet, especially if they reach you. Accept them and ask for help whenever required.

- **Protect yourself**: From your child's first birthday party to their graduation, from their first day of school to their first day at work, your mind would, consciously and unconsciously, be focused on their life. Do not keep your health on the back burner. Get enough sun, maintain your nutrition, watch your favorite shows, exercise well, stay hydrated, and go out and meet people whenever possible.

- **Laugh more**: They were not wrong when they said, "laughter is the best medicine." It indeed is. It promotes good health, allows healthy hormones to relieve stress, and relaxes the body and mind. Find reasons to be happy. Appreciate nature. Be with people who make you smile, and deliberately cut out those from life who can negatively influence you and your family.

ADHD gives a lot of potential to other realms of life. People who have done well in life can thank this condition. This includes creative people, thinkers, theorists, chefs, athletes, businesspeople, and many others. As a parent, instead of viewing the greener grass on the other side, maybe it is time that you water your own grass. Your child is no less than anyone else; this is a truth you must remind yourself of, especially on difficult days. And truth be told, there will be many tough days. Make sure you first take care of yourself and then face them.

DAVID NEELEMAN AND HIS SOARING SUCCESS

The founder of JetBlue Airways, David Neeleman, once said that he would choose ADHD over a normal life. Neeleman does not take any medication. Neeleman believes that his disorganization, lack of clarity and focus, and procrastination resulted in the gift of creativity. This creativity was combined with his risk-taking ability, which finally made him what he is today. When he said he wanted to give New York the new, low-fare hometown airline, everyone from the venture capitalists who refused to invest in his plan to the media shook their heads. But Neeleman believed in himself when others did not, just as his parents had believed in him when his teachers had not. He knew that he could find simple solutions to complicated problems. He believed in himself and his ever-evolving curiosity to make things better. He owes this curiosity to ADHD. Yes, his personal life is not this perfect. Because he has so much on his mind, his family is always at a loss as to what is next. But he believes this is what keeps his life balanced and interesting. He is not into mundane activities. To control his mind, he has surrounded himself with a team he trusts. However, he is still the same man who keeps his wallet and keys together to not lose them. He needs reminders for appointments. Despite all this, he feels that these are little negatives that he has to trade off for considerable profits. He did not let an untreated ADHD condition discourage or fail him.

9

HELPING YOUR CHILD SUCCEED IN SCHOOL

We already saw that the confidence of parents can hit a new low when the child suffers. From my personal experience, I may convincingly say that showing your child your happy face is extremely hard because that is not the emotion you wake up with every morning. Instead of acting out a facade, it is better to seek help and help yourself out of the situation. It may take a long time but trying in small steps and succeeding in even smaller steps is much better than lying to yourself and your child. To help your child succeed at every major turn of their life, parents need to succeed in boosting their confidence while facing everyday struggles.

ADHD: HOW TO HELP YOUR CHILD AT SCHOOL

Many children have subtle signs of ADHD. These signs become more pronounced when they start attending school. Again, it is diagnosed more easily in boys than in girls. The inability to pay attention, follow instructions, sit still for too long, make new friends, and concentrate on a task becomes more apparent once the child begins attending school. These kids have special needs in the classroom, just like they do at home. Getting them to do any work at school will be as difficult as getting them ready for school. Many teachers who are not aware of this may get impatient and upset. The following things need to be clarified to the teacher:

- The child is not ignoring instructions because they are insolent. They are not disobeying or defying rules.
- They are not lazy or stupid.
- Any unexpected change or event at school may greatly upset them.
- Their distraction is not an insult to the teacher or their teaching methods.

Sending a Piece of Home to School

To increase your kid's chance of success, you need to be confident about your parenting. Your nervousness will not help your child; your conviction will. You may be in touch with the child. You may also keep yourself updated with every piece of information that comes your way. But the real secret lies in accepting your reality and not overanalyzing the situation. You have to treat your child normally. At the same time, what you teach them at home is what they take to school. Let us look at some fun ways that you can be with your child about their values without being physically present to check on them.

- **Be the role model that they need**: Teach them about strength, not physical, but mental. You may feel this is the wrong advice for someone with a young kid, but training begins at home. Set realistic but fun family rules and enforce them with consistency. These could be about healthy eating habits, greeting elders and being respectful, keeping the hands clean, brushing the teeth twice daily, and having a fixed time to watch television. This tells the kid, from very early on, that not everything is at their disposal. Every activity has extremes, and there are limits that they must not cross. They must know that every action has a consequence. Early age is the best to teach how to differentiate wrong from right. You can use colors, figures, storybooks, and rewards for familiarizing kids with routines. Set routines help in reducing stress and maintaining a balance. Healthy family bonds strengthens these routines.

- **Building relationships**: No matter how shy or hyperactive your child is, it is necessary to teach them the values of love and warmth. When a child grows up in a happy and healthy environment, it is easier to educate them about kindness, gratitude, forgiveness, honesty, and love. These values teach resilience and tolerance. These values make it easier for the child to be around other kids in an alien environment. Loving, sharing, caring, and helping begin at home.
- **Communicate**: Be in constant communication with their teacher. You may discuss strategies and share valuable insights.
- **Ask them to ask for help**: Teach your kids to ask for help whenever needed. Most teachers would happily and proactively help the child.
- **Good sleep**: Children and teenagers with ADHD must have a proper sleep of 8 hours. It

helps the brain relax and be ready for the next day's routine. All screens must be turned off two hours before bedtime. Bedtime reading is a good habit to calm their ADHD mind.

- **Healthy eating**: Balance their sugar and salt intake. Home-cooked, healthy food is preferred over takeout and junk food.
- **Clear and concise rules**: The teacher must be made aware of the child's situation. Just as at home, the school rules must be consistent, with having kids repeat them after the teacher. This is important to help kids transition from one activity to another. Timers, bells, signals, cues, etc., may help the child understand when to stop and when to begin again. These tricks teach time management and discipline. Some rules can be flexible. When too restless, a child with ADHD must be allowed to stand in their place for a while. They can be asked to move around the class to distribute handouts. They can also be allowed to keep a Koosh ball with themselves to have something to hold on to instead of disturbing the entire class. This Koosh ball can accompany the child at home to have a sense of security in the child's mind. Again, fixed screen time with playtime at home regulates body and mind function.

- **Appreciation**: Just as rewards remind a child of their good results and the path they need to keep choosing, words of appreciation, kind remarks, and positive feedback by the teacher on a child's progress can encourage them greatly. This creates a positive environment for the child.

- **End distractions**: Pencil sharpeners, talkative classmates, and even an open window may easily distract an unsettled mind. White blank walls, no music or noise, the considerable distance between kids' seats, and minimum articles on the desk to fidget with are one way to gather a child's attention. Such kids can also be seated in the front, close to the teacher, to have their full attention.

- **Breaks**: Small breaks can help kids focus better. They can interact with other kids, drink water, or simply relax before they need to be attentive again. This teaches them to tame their diversion and keep the trail of thoughts intact.

- **Limit information**: Information overload can be disturbing for small kids. Their minds are like blank slates. The information must always be poured into the mind drop-by-drop or the class may get overwhelming, boring, and even repulsive for some kids.

- **Support groups in schools**: If the school has a therapist or social support group, they may immediately take care of the child in case of extra help. With the information gathered, the kid may be paired up with a friendlier and more helpful kid. This company may help the kid with ADHD to focus better in class, improve social behavior, and shed inhibitions.

- **Behavior classroom management**: The child may be encouraged in PTAs and be given constructive feedback. Lessons that involve motor functions and the brain (for example, poetry recitals with actions) stimulate the brain and allow them to be physically active as well.

- **Leniency**: Scoring methods must be lenient and flexible both at home and in the classroom. Grades must not demoralize the child, but their purpose must be to find the hidden talent of the child. A fair and friendly scoring system can motivate the child better than the chocolates they may get as rewards. Children are like flowers that bloom in different environments. To help them thrive, we cannot keep them in boxes.

- **Skill building**: The habit of organizing things begins at home. The child must have a sense of time, space, deadlines, and calendars as they grow up. Smaller things like arranging your articles, organizing the books, placing blocks in accordance with their increasing size, trying and opening knots, and allowing every child to speak in front of the class may ameliorate their skill-learning capabilities. Presence of mind, organizing things, and loud and clear speech are just some skills that can be taught from a very early age. This coupled with therapy and counseling can implant positive behavior in the child.

- **Wise choice**: Choose the school that has special programs, resources, and trained staff for kids with ADHD. Working closely with the staff and teachers may help create an effective plan for the child.

AN ADHD SUCCESS STORY

Scott Taylor got a Certificate of Academic Excellence from the Canadian Psychological Association in 2018 for his research on attention-deficit/hyperactivity disorder, executive functions, and putting things off. What very few knew was that this was Scott's personal story. This research was the sum of his experiences as a child, then a student, and, in the later part, a success.

His ADHD was diagnosed when he was a kid. He remembers his struggles with symptoms. He remembers how his neurodevelopmental disorder compromised his focus, energy, and control. He also remembers how he differed from his peers due to functions like time management, memorizing stuff, finishing homework, and regulating emotions. These are the primary symptoms of ADHD because they distinguish any child from other children their age.

However, by implementing strategies and resources in multiple areas of his life, he was able to overcome his executive functional disorder and achieve success. Today, he sits back and observes his life, coming to regard ADHD as an advantage, a strength, and a blessing. It made him want to study child psychology and help children of the next generation with their complicated needs in a simple way.

He believes that once an individual chooses their career path, their ADHD does not act as a hurdle, although it may push them toward excellence. Albert Einstein, John F. Kennedy, Sir Richard Branson, and Michael Jordan, to name a few.

Taylor's hyperactive condition also earned him the "class clown" title. It was common for the troublemaker to get into trouble. And today, as someone who understands all this, it worries him for all the other children who are told that they are staring down a dark path with this behavior. Today, when he looks back on his journey, he sees that it was full of obstacles but also of opportunities that needed to be taken. He, too, thought that darkness awaited him. But he did not let any of the impairments dim the light from his life.

I would like to bring something to the parents' attention here. Just like any other kid, kids with ADHD are also vulnerable to the ugly side of the world that we live in. Just because these kids function slightly differently, they do not deserve stricter restrictions or extra reminders. They need to be treated like other children. Antisocial behavior, failing grades, violence, and substance abuse are evils of society that leave cues, and these cues have a major role in protecting the child. But the idea that "ADHD equals bad outcomes" is false.

Taylor also saw the cues and made the right turn at the right time. He could see that his teenage self was not going down the desired path. What others saw as adversity; he saw as an opportunity. Like most people who have succeeded with ADHD, Taylor was also told by his teachers and counselors that he would not attain anything in life. They told him that he may earn a college diploma, but he did not have a lot of options in life to choose from. His dream of attending college was not to be taken seriously. He was told that his peers and professors would not help him out even if he made it to college. To put that in perspective, the people who were supposed to guide and help him discouraged him with a straight no. His resilience did not let him give up so easily. Finally, he did attend college.

This world was different, and everything was new, yes, but it also gave him a fresh start. He was not the class clown or the hyperactive child here. This world gave him another chance to just be himself and not be seen through the lens of prejudice. On the contrary, he made friends and found genuine support in this phase of life.

University life also taught him special skills to not only counter his ADHD disadvantages but also push him toward better outcomes.

He also dissects the stigma that surrounds medication. Medication is necessary, and it acts gradually. There have been times when he felt low, and people around him joked and inquired if he took his medications. ADHD is a lot more than the expressions on the face. It has a lot to do with the mind, which controls the body and emotions. Most of the time, it is an incomprehensible situation a child faces, coupled with the stigma surrounding their behavior and actions. This stigma is powerful, causing the child to fold inward like a flower beginning to wilt. ADHD is not associated with medication as a disease because ADHD is not a disease.

Society must understand this because temperament has a heavier bearing on a child than their own condition. He believes that medication and cognitive-behavioral therapy (CBT) played a significant role in his current success.

As his future grew and he saw more possibilities, Taylor also broke the shackles of stigma. It was a phase of self-discovery. Before, he couldn't work well because of his impulses, long-term procrastination, behavioral over-whelm, and impatience. He was now concentrating on self-care and long-term goals. His role models include his teachers, professors, and mentors.

It took a long time, and it was a long journey, but encouragement from family and friends, the right guidance, skills, strategies, exercise, therapy, and medication helped him choose the brighter path. This, along with his perseverance, grit, honesty, and dedication, refused to accompany any reluctance or negativity.

SUPPORTING YOUR CHILD
AT HOME

Throughout the book, I have covered certain tips on how to be there for your child who has ADHD. Every day is a constant battle. The secret lies in treating the situation as normal. Normal does not mean overlooking the problems; normal means accepting that your family's situation is not abnormal.

You will have to support your child at each step while being your own biggest support on the journey.

Your home's environment should be harmonious; your routines should be healthy; your schedules must be well-planned and accommodate everyone's concerns; and your positive feedback to the child must be genuine.

This chapter summarizes these tips to help you parent gently, mindfully, and efficiently.

SUPPORT, NOT SUGARCOAT

ADHD symptoms can greatly vary from case to case. The parent's response to the child's condition can either improve or worsen these symptoms. There is only so much you can learn from the world around you. No one tests you better than reality. If your child has been diagnosed with ADHD, then you can do the following to be more involved:

Work closely with your child's teachers and therapist:

- **Have a clear set of goals**: You should know what you want from your child. Your goal should be their betterment, not your need to prove anything to anyone. For example, encouraging healthy eating habits or sleeping on time could be two goals you want to focus on for now. For this, you will have to make their diet healthier by adding fruits, vegetables, whole grains, and lean protein to it. For better sleep, you need to remove their distractions and make sure they sleep for at least ten hours. You would have to adjust your schedule accordingly and model good behavior in front of them to encourage it.

- **Give uncomplicated instructions**: Your instructions must be simple, regularly repeated, and short. They can be written in color, have pictures and diagrams to help explain, and must be important. Your child must understand the purpose of each rule and task.

- **Cut out distraction**: Video games, phones, computers, and television must have a limited designated time. Inculcate healthier activities like reading, writing, music, gardening, and painting.

- **Encourage outdoor activities**: You must encourage physical activities and outdoor events, especially in natural and green settings. It helps improve focus and concentration in children and reduces the severity of their ADHD symptoms. A minimum of 45 to 60 minutes of an active lifestyle that includes running, swimming, playing any sport, or riding a bike can be very helpful.

- **Set a proper routine**: Involve them when making rules of the house and tell them clearly what behavior is expected of them. Use reminders and simple instructions to keep them engaged. Deadlines must be introduced, and consistency must be checked. They must have breaks in between activities.

- **Join social support groups**: Suh groups may help you cope with your child's condition. It can help your child make new friends. Experience sharing can be a very helpful and reassuring activity.

- **Be patient**: You need to be patient with your child because they may need extra time to accomplish a task. Your visible anger and frustration can spur negative reactions in your child. Your mindfulness and calmness can keep them calm as well.

- **Be supportive of your child**: Praise your child when they do something well and offer them help when you see them struggling. Have positive interactions with them. Encourage their friendship with other children of their age. Explore their interest and enroll them in a class or activity club of their choice. Do not keep them around people who give negative feedback. Avoid negative emotions or reinforcement like scolding, complaining, or punishment.

ANOTHER LIFE: THE STORY OF GRACE

At the age of 42, Grace was diagnosed with ADHD. Today, she recalls her childhood. She says that had it been diagnosed at an early age, her life would have been very difficult, especially her childhood.

Although slow, Grace was never picked on for falling behind. She feels she was fortunate to learn at her own pace. Every time it felt like she was falling behind, she got the right help. She excelled in math. It came naturally to her because it made her curious. Reading was difficult for her. Had it not been for her first-grade teacher, who did not give up on her, she would have learned it quite late. Middle school and high school were difficult for her, even when she had friends. Her intelligence could not push up her grades. Each semester began with a lot of enthusiasm and optimism, but she fell behind as the time passed. The first reason was procrastination. The second was her anxiety. Thirdly, her symptoms were getting worse, making her mentally exhausted. Fourthly, it was difficult for her to follow instructions. This story continued throughout her college and graduate studies. She was forced to take a year off. While she graduated in the second year, she took twice as long as her peers did. She had to repeat classes that helped her learn and relearn everything. Soon after, she had a nervous breakdown.

When she was diagnosed with OCD, she started taking medicines. For over two decades, she had been striving for perfection while taking medicines. She was running after an invisible goal, a perfectly imperfect drama, pushing her limits of capacity and sanity. Today, she feels that had her diagnosis been done correctly at the right time, she would not have been so worn out after struggling for years. Her parents (mom, a professor of education, and dad, a psychotherapist) were extremely disturbed and shocked to hear of her diagnosis.

Some parents miss the sign, but here is the key take-away from this story: not all ADHD cases are similar. Today, Grace understands herself better. Her ADHD was never the problem; its elusive nature and the wrong diagnosis were.

11

SELF-CARE FOR PARENTS

A DHD is present in 8.5% of all children, and in most cases, it is first identified in older school-going children when they struggle with schoolwork and socialization. While it is more easily diagnosed in boys than in girls, they both equally tend to have ADHD. Boys tend to show more signs of hyperactivity. Girls, on the other hand, do not externalize signs and are more inactive.

The American Academy of Pediatrics says that parents, teachers, and other adults who care for the child could try "watchful waiting" for about 10 weeks and keep an eye on the child's symptoms. This watchful waiting sometimes turns into watchful testing and trying, and ultimately, watchful punishment.

WHY SELF-CARE IS IMPORTANT FOR PARENTS OF KIDS WITH ADHD?

Self-care must be very important for parents because they forget to take care of themselves. It is often overlooked because parents are busy taking care of their kids with ADHD. When I explain this to parents who discuss their constant fatigue and unenthusiasm, I try to explain to them the ways to not be burned out. In this chapter, I explain why parents must take care of themselves emotionally and physically to take better care of their children.

What Is Self-Care?

Everyone keeps talking about self-care, but very few know its real meaning. Self-care is not just about pampering yourself after some heavy days. Self-care is also about treating yourself well. For parents, it is about keeping aside the rewarding days and taking into consideration the busy, stressful, and dismissive days. From social media posts to articles written by medical professionals, everyone is asking parents to take some breaks for their self-care. But parents often feel that this respite from the schedule is selfish and unnecessary.

Self-care is about making your needs a priority. This does not make a parent selfish; it makes them human. You are not doing anything that puts your child in danger; you are saving yourself from bad health. This care is not self-absorption. It is self-liberation. It is a way for parents to understand how they can balance life with responsibilities.

Why Does Self-Care Matter?

Once the significance of the balance between living your life and managing your responsibilities is realized, parents will see how enriching it can be.

Self-care, or caring about oneself, has many aspects, the most important of which is showcasing kindness to oneself and a practical approach to goals. One cannot be emotionally attached to goals and overwork to attain unrealistic results. That will always lead to disappointment. Instead, one must follow the quality over quantity approach. For example, it does not matter how many hours you spend with your child; it is about the memories you create with them. This also rejects the idea of sacrificing your social life because you are raising a kid with ADHD. In fact, the right work-play (yes, parents need some relaxation too) will help you deal with the challenges better. It helps you stay calmer, more mindful, present, and more patient. It is also extremely important to recognize and counter the signs of burnout. Some common signs of burnout are:

- fatigue
- anxiety
- irritation
- anger
- lack of sleep
- impatience
- tension
- unhealthy eating habits

The well-being of parents affects the well-being of their children. As parents of kids with ADHD, your responsibilities increase with the constant hyperactivity and inactivity around you. In addition to this, you also have to remember and keep up with medication and therapy schedules, manage the emotional, mental, and physical needs of your child, and deal with teachers, doctors, behavior therapists, and psychologists. Amidst all this, you have to maintain some semblance of a normal life and not be continuously overwhelmed.

When there is too much on the plate, sometimes it's okay to keep the plate down.

Benefits of Practicing Self-Care

It is better to take a step back and realize that as a parent, your mental, emotional, and physical health are closely related to how you treat yourself with love and care instead of craving some alone time while stuck in a busy and tiring moment.

Ask yourself an honest question, "Do I need some time to accept this?" and you shall get the right answer. Apart from many unprepared moments of enlightenment, you would also come across the "oh, I wish I knew this before!" moments. Self-care is the only way to keep you sane through this journey.

- **Preventing burnout**: Burnout happens when you are constantly working. One task completed, a few more to go, and before you realize it, this chain of chores becomes never ending. Breakfast, school drop off, laundry, lunch, evening sports practice, therapy, dinner, homework, doing the dishes, and whatnot? Sooner or later, you will feel ignored by yourself. Remind yourself that it is not selfish to sometimes put yourself before others. There are a few ways to prevent this state. Firstly, try to plan your day. Secondly, make sure you sleep well. Thirdly, take out some time for an activity that you truly enjoy. Lastly, do not feel inadequate in asking for help. Distribute chores wisely so that you do not burden yourself with too much. Burnout also comes with other signs and symptoms. You may see your eating and sleeping habits changing. You may get upset, anxious, or feel unhappy and unsafe. You may feel tired and irritated. You may find it difficult to concentrate. You may also have headaches, body pain, dizziness, or stomach upset.

- **Maintaining health**: Many parents with kids who have ADHD tell me that they feel too tired to take care of themselves. Only when you are serious about your health will you be able to maintain it well. You need to avoid burnout and learn to take smaller breaks. Staying hydrated and having smaller meals are recommended. Make sure you take your vitamins and supplements on time. Physical exercise is known to be a great stress reliever as it releases endorphins. Stress, low immunity, tiredness, lack of sleep, and improper meals can make you more susceptible to sickness. This is something you cannot afford as a parent.

- **Setting a good example for your kids**: Parents are whom their kids look up to. To set a good example for kids, parents must practice what they preach and control their emotions. Kids with ADHD find it greatly hindering following and sticking to routines. For this, the parents must have a set routine that they should try to stick to. This routine must also have elements of self-care. This way, the kids would also learn to care for themselves. Your healthy boundaries and effective coping mechanisms like meditation, exercise, spending time with loved ones, hobbies, and interests will set up an example that teaches them to face stress and disorder with routine, resilience, recreation, and rest.

- **Setting healthy boundaries**: Your conduct will teach the child that it is acceptable to have healthy boundaries. For this, you first need to define healthy boundaries for yourself, personally and professionally. Know your commitments and responsibilities and try not to be guilty about "not being able to do more." Do not see yourself as an unstoppable force. See yourself as a human being with personal space and needs. You can be clear to your children about what you expect from them. For example, their behavior, their dedication, and their honesty. Your being firm does not compromise your love for them. You also need to maintain healthy boundaries with friends, relatives, colleagues, and even your extended family members.

- **Healthy for your marriage**: As a parent of a kid with ADHD, you will be required to take tough decisions and exercise thorough care. With constant redirection, interjection, and anticipation about the next moment, you may not always be your best self. This is when your partner needs to step up and act like your team member. Similarly, when they feel low and lost, it is your job to step up. You both cannot function in isolation. This is a journey of two codependents who would need recovery and nourishing breaks from time to time. Self-care allows parents to be better focused and be more positive and balanced. It helps two individuals to have a stronger bond when they are dealing with their child's ADHD. It is these layers that absorb the negativity and promote kindness and connection between them.

Ideas for Practicing Self-Care

There are a few ways to make sure you take good care of yourself as a parent:

- **Get enough sleep**: You cannot work continuously for 12 hours and ignore your sleep. Do not overwork your body and mind. A sound sleep of 6–8 hours is a minimum necessity and can give you magical results when stress, tough decision-making, and focus are involved.
- **Ask for help**: Parents often tell me that they do not know how to connect to others for help. They often know the sources, and they have supportive friends and family, but "something" pulls them back. This could be a false feeling of self-sufficiency, guilt, fear of false perception, ego, or fear of rejection. I would say, try to cross these hurdles and ask for help at the required time.
- **Stick to the routine**: It is very important to stick to a routine to not feel spent. Try disturbing your routine for one day and you will see the spill-over effects in the next week. It comes as a chain reaction. I am not saying you cannot take a break and do something

different. But a routine allows you and your child with ADHD to have healthier discipline. This discipline is a form of self-care.

- **Do not ignore your interests**: Self-care is not selfish. You cannot be stagnant as a human being. You need to be the seed that gets planted and grows. You can only provide care when you have learned to provide care for yourself.

- **Keep an eye on yourself**: Watch how you speak to or think about yourself. Little thoughts matter a lot. What do you think when you see yourself in the mirror or how do you treat yourself when you fail to solve a problem?

- **Have realistic expectations**: Do not expect your efforts to produce instant desirable results. Recognize all efforts, even the smallest ones.

- **Avoid drinking and smoking**: These vices will not only bring your energy down, but they also have nothing positive to contribute to your emotional, mental, or physical health or life, rather, they may make you restless and anxious.

- **Keep your calm**: Meditation, exercise, painting, musing, hiking, or spending time in nature are great ways to maintain your calm. Do take regular breaks from daily chores and responsibilities. Maintain healthy boundaries to protect yourself.

You do not have to be conceited in the manner in which you approach parenthood and refuse to see any gaps. Be proud of the parent you are, but do not be proud of sacrificing. You owe yourself some care, affection, and quality time.

12

SEEKING PROFESSIONAL HELP

A child with ADHD can be challenging to deal with. It could also be confusing—the signs, the actions, the solutions, and the progress. Seeking help at any juncture can be a natural call. A lot of parents raising kids with ADHD, hesitate at such crucial moments because:

- They have a lack of trust for a third person's intervention.
- They can deal with their child the best.
- They want to go the traditional way and wait for the results before seeking help.

It is difficult to know exactly when things will improve. The way to therapy, behavioral help, and advancement does not come with an expiration date. One needs to pay close attention to every small detail. Parents are the first to bear this responsibility for their ADHD child. Some details can be missed or misread. But ultimately, it is their call to decide what is good for the child and what is not.

Signs can leave you wondering: Is there more to this? Is my child less distracted because they are more focused and enjoying their work? Is this temporary? Is my child's disinterest because the task or subject is uninteresting to them? Or is it the same with everything that they try to do?

Kids can be energetic, distracted, forgetful, and extremely talkative or overtly shy. Documenting their behavior is a great way to learn about slight differences. You may want to:

- video record it
- have a journal for it to take notes
- have routines and timings check your kid's reaction to decorum, discipline, and instructions
- notice their behavior toward warnings
- observe their curiosity or disinterest and talk to them about it

ARE YOU A FAILURE AS A PARENT IF YOU SEEK HELP?

This is probably the biggest fear of any parent. While Darla was trying her best to look for answers, Matt was by her side. Although a small part of him was worried about "not being there enough" for their child, since the early days of Darla's pregnancy, Matt had always been present. He was often complimented for being extremely caring, loving, loyal, and attentive. For a first-time dad, he went out of his way to do his home-work. However, at this point, no matter how many sources he had researched and investigated from, he had the feeling that things were slipping out of his hands. Blogs, vlogs, articles, research papers, books, and interviews—you name it, Matt was starving for signs that could bring him closer to his son. He had all the information he needed in his head, but he was not very sure about how to use it.

The quintessential tenacity with which Matt and Darla were handling everything was admired by everyone who saw them. Even as they struggled, they held on tightly. But sometimes, we need to loosen the grip on the situation in order to explore more. The idea that letting go is the same as losing power is false and has no basis in fact. It can get messy while raising a kid with ADHD. Parents are prone to make tons of mistakes. Conversations with your child who suffers from ADHD can get difficult at times. But just because they are fidgety, that does not mean they cannot look you in the eye and demand what they want. If you teach them about the fine line between right and wrong, they will understand it. Similarly, you need to understand the fine line between efficiency and redundancy. Asking for help does not reduce your efficiency as a parent.

There are many internal and external barriers that people encounter when they are seeking help for their child. One is culture. The world around us is painted perfect. Be it the photos on social media or the advertisements on TV. How much of what we watch or follow is ADHD-friendly? This is a blissful disservice since the world around us is not flawless but forces us to bust the myth around perfection. In this culture, even the slightest variations are regarded as flaws.

The second barrier is shame. This is a fallout from the previous barrier. Because a false enigma surrounds perfection, people fail to accept themselves as they are. They think their reality will bring shame upon them. Imagine how cruel the world would be if it did not let people be themselves. This is a crisis adult have that passes down to their children as well. In a world of brutal competition, anything that pulls one back is seen as a shame. We get addicted to shame more than we should given the efforts we must make to save ourselves from it.

The third barrier is expectations. There is a social cost people need to pay to accept their flaws. Sadly, we attach these false dictums even to children who are too little to understand them. Even before a child is born, we start having expectations and fantasies. Our dreams are about our children's security. Our world is centered around their needs and upbringing. When a child has special needs, not all couples are mentally and emotionally prepared for special responsibilities.

The fourth barrier is regarding mental health. The dichotomy of mental health versus mental disorder is blurred for many. People think you can either be mentally fit or mentally unfit. Any disorder is seen as being at the extreme end of the spectrum. People feel that their kids may have a shortcoming due to ADHD, which can actually be their strength.

A **tip for parents** would be to keep aside prejudices about the world and fears about themselves and observe the child with a neutral perspective. Watch them play, keep an eye on their interests, allow yourself to understand their experience and see the world through your child's eyes, and let them make small troubles. In their social nourishment lies the story that is weaving in their heads. To be an anchor to that story, we must listen to their narration.

Sometimes, despite being the anchor, you may need an interpreter for their story. Do not expect yourself to understand everything that happens in your child's brain. The job of this interpreter is to help you anchor the story better. This is the help you need because you may struggle to keep up with your child's pace. Do not let this dim your light or make you doubt your abilities as a parent.

Signs That You Need to Seek Help

There could be various signs that direct you to the understanding that you must ask for help. These are:

- inability to cope with your child
- deteriorating mental health
- the feeling of handling everything alone
- too much pressure
- no longer proper communication with your child
- your child's progress stalling or declining
- ineffective discipline strategies
- worsening social behavior of your child
- immaturity defying the age of your child
- any indication of self-harm in your child

PROFESSIONALS WHO MAY HELP YOU

When you need help for your child, the first person you should call is your general practitioner (GP), family doctor, or pediatrician. These are the people who may have an idea about your family's history. If your child has been diagnosed with ADHD and the symptoms (that we saw in Chapters 1 and 2) tell a true tale, you may need continuous medical attention for your child. This team of professionals may include a few of the following:

- **Pediatricians**: These are doctors who assess the condition of your child and evaluate the symptoms. They prescribe medicines and observe reactions to these medicines. They try to keep in check the negative impacts of ADHD. They could be found at health centers, clinics, and hospitals.
- **Psychologists**: These are experts in psychology and help diagnose and treat mental, emotional, and behavioral issues. They are trained for diagnosis and therapy but are not allowed to prescribe medicines.
- **Psychiatrists for children and adolescents**: To diagnose and help deal with associated mental health issues that may accompany ADHD, like

depression, anxiety, and nervousness. They are medical professionals capable of prescribing drugs for the same.

- **Therapists**: Therapists or counselors have knowledge beyond the working knowledge of the general psyche. These people understand the mental, emotional, and behavioral needs of the human mind. They can offer a unique perspective on the problem and may offer counseling sessions where one can be as they are without fear of prejudice. These professionals are not allowed to prescribe drugs.

- **Neurologists**: Pediatric neurologists are medical doctors specializing in the evaluation and diagnosis of mental or behavioral disorders. They prescribe medicines and examine results. They detect disorders of the nervous system and other neurodevelopmental issues.

- **Speech therapists**: They help with spoken or written language. Speech therapists help to correct the speech. Other skills can be corrected by occupational therapists.

- **Nurses**: Nurses are medical assistants working under the supervision of senior and qualified medical professionals. They are not doctors but can work under the doctor's guidance. They can also be the first attendees to your child, may note down the immediate symptoms, can do the initial diagnosis for the doctor to look into, and can prescribe medicines with the doctor's permission.

- **Physician Assistants or PAs**: Their job is to conduct tests and run scans. They can diagnose and help the doctor with treatment. They work under professional guidance and can write prescriptions under the physician's supervision.

- **Social workers**: Social workers have a social role. Their organizations and support may help in education, training, conditioning, and providing tips to both the child and the parents to develop skills to better deal with ADHD and not let it be an impairment in life. They are qualified for clinical social work. They can be approached at any or all stages of the journey. They are mostly approached in schools or mental health clinics.

ADHD diagnosis, care, and treatment may involve several steps. At every step, a qualified professional has a role to play. Pediatricians, physicians, licensed therapists and counselors, and nurses have a role to play in your child's treatment. These professionals have a better chance of understanding your situation because they may have experience dealing with similar cases. Their guidance and advice may be meaningful because they can help you deal with your child's tantrums or make them focus better. This team also includes medical professionals, who can also prescribe the right medication.

Yet not all of them are medically qualified to prescribe medication for your child. Medications cannot be prescribed without thorough evaluations. It is very important that you are involved and told what is going on at every step of the questioning, evaluation, and treatment. The professionals must also keep communicating with each other to exchange information and make steady progress. On the other hand, your child must be comfortable with the professional team and must trust them.

Each of these professionals has an area of expertise. You have to find a team that you and your child are comfortable with. You can understand your child better with their understanding of the situation, and you can come up with a feasible plan to help the child.

CHOOSING THE RIGHT PROFESSIONALS

To find a certain comfort level that your child can share with the professional dealing with them, we need to consider a few things. A **reminder for parents** would be that every team you choose will have pros and cons. You have to weigh them to get the best results for your child. Each professional has a unique role to play. Sometimes a unidirectional treatment line may not help, and a combination of treatment methods is recommended. This is why we need a comprehensive analysis of your child's situation. There are a few things that can be considered during this quest for the perfect team:

- **Qualification**: Make sure the professionals are well qualified, trustworthy, and with a distinguished reputation. For this, you may check their previous records.
- **Approach**: The right approach always tries to first rule out the possibilities of other disorders causing the symptoms.
- **Referrals**: A primary care doctor can diagnose ADHD, but they may also refer your child's case to a specialist. Your doctor may also refer the case to a psychiatrist or a psychologist depending on the needs of your child.

- **Cost**: The cost of ADHD treatment could form a significant share of the family's income. This cost could also affect the ability of many families to afford the treatment. Treatment from ADHD specialists can be costly, and not all costs are covered under insurance.

There are organizations and resource centers at local and national levels that offer valuable information and support in the form of books, audio recordings, podcasts, articles, and brochures.

Make sure to make use of the assessment checklist present in the ADHD toolkit, which is available online and offline. This toolkit, prepared by the American Academy of Pediatrics, can help you assess the ADHD tools your doctor uses. This is necessary because doctors have a wide range when it comes to expertise and the tools that they use. Any additional referral may incur a special cost.

A thorough examination of your child for ADHD, learning disabilities, and other psychological issues qualifies them for accommodations and interventions by the school provided by federal law.

Some clinical services are provided free of charge or on a sliding scale. Some have insurance plans; others have treatment guided by mentors.

It can be painful to see your child in pain. On some days, this can be extremely draining. This is when parents need to understand that they cannot handle everything on their own. It is okay to seek help. There is no weakness in that. It is, in fact, necessary to seek help, not only for your child's sake but for your own. The right guidance can help you, which in turn will allow you to help your child. You can do it your way. You have to follow the instructions, but with constant communication with and advice from your child's therapist, you can make minute changes that personalize your experience with your child. See this as a training process and not as losing control over the situation. You are still in charge of your child, despite looking for answers elsewhere.

Your curiosity (and sometimes desperation) to seek answers proves that you care, and that is all that matters.

13

ADHD TREATMENTS

There are treatment methods for ADHD that do not require medication. Yes, you read that right. There are non-medication treatment methods for ADHD that, depending on the case, can be just as effective as medicines.

THE KEY ELEMENTS OF AN EFFECTIVE TREATMENT PLAN

Edward Hallowell, a certified child and adult psychiatrist and a well-known name in the field of ADHD, founded the Hallowell ADHD Centers, which have locations throughout the United States. He has been in the field for the past four decades and is also a best-selling author with various books to his name. His strength-based approach to dealing with neurodiversity, as well as his groundbreaking distraction series, sparked a new conversation about ADHD. According to him, there are four key elements of an effective ADHD treatment plan:

- **Education**: Education helps the parents to understand their child's condition better. Learning, talking, and investigating about it is fascinating because what we see as our child's problems can be their strengths. As I mentioned before as well, not all ADHD cases are similar. Every case has unique signs and symptoms which are not its weaknesses. More awareness and information allow the parent to be better equipped with the situation and look for the right treatment.
- **Therapy**: Behavior therapy or coaching strengthens the chances of your child's survival. These are strategies to help tackle different situations. Parallel therapy for parents teaches them to deal better with the child's changing behavior that comes with ADHD. It is the light that shows the way when things get tough.
- **Medication**: Medication is often prescribed with therapy in cases where therapy alone does not work. It is effective in helping the child

focus better. Many parents reach out to me because they have doubts regarding medication. I believe parents can monitor medicines for kids. Since these are only to be taken as prescribed, there should be no miscalculation. Adolescents may also follow different weekly and weekend plans, have medicines only before exams, or participate in competitive performances and events. This can be discussed with the physician.

- **Support**: Support, emotional and mental, comes from the community and whom we decide to surround ourselves with. For kids with ADHD, their parents, family, friends, teachers, and therapists form this immediate support group. The other families experiencing the same, online resources, and bits of advice from psychologists, pediatrics, and psychiatrists are always helpful.

MEDICATIONS FOR ADHD

ADHD medication helps improve the work of neuro-transmitters in the brain. These, in turn, reduce hyper-activity, increase attention span and focus, manage the executive functioning of the body, and reduce impulsive behavior. These medications affect kids differently.

What may work for one person may not work for another. Your doctor will try various medications and dosages to see which one works best for your child.

Different Types of ADHD Medications

Stimulants

These are the most common types of ADHD prescription medications. They increase dopamine and norepinephrine in the brain, which help people pay more attention, think clearly, and stay motivated. These stimulants could be short-term, whose effects may last up to 4 hours, or long-term, whose effects may last up to 16 hours. Two categories of stimulants are methylphenidates (Ritalin) and amphetamines (Adderall).

Non-Stimulants

These elevate the norepinephrine levels in the brain but may take longer than stimulants to start working. The full effects of these medications are felt when taken regularly for weeks. Common non-stimulant medications used to treat ADHD include atomoxetine (Strattera) and guanfacine (Intuniv).

Antidepressants

These are not FDA-approved for ADHD treatment, but doctors may prescribe them alone or in combination with stimulants. These are mostly the most common drug classes are norepinephrine-dopamine reuptake inhibitors and tricyclics.

Risks and Side Effects of ADHD Medication

There are a few risks and side effects with these medicines. One must consult the doctor immediately if these get severe.

- weight loss
- sleep problems
- irritation
- appetite loss
- anxiety
- rebound effect
- fatigue
- dry mouth
- nausea
- constipation
- sweating

14

THERAPY FOR ADHD

There are various kinds of therapies for children suffering from ADHD. For obvious reasons, the therapies that are in place for kids with ADHD have some extra sensitive and attentive elements. Different therapy methods involve different steps and elements. Note that one does not "grow out" of ADHD. There is no cure for ADHD, but there are several effective therapy methods to mellow the impacts of symptoms acting as a barrier to a successful life. Every therapy helps the individual master the art of living with ADHD without it becoming a barrier in their life. This chapter explores various therapy methods for children dealing with ADHD. You will come across the significance and effectiveness of each therapy while learning about its pros and cons.

DIFFERENT KINDS OF THERAPY

There is no one type of therapy at your disposal. A consultation with a medical professional whose expertise lies in mental and behavioral health will help you determine what type of therapy would suit your child the best. This is the first step toward managing ADHD symptoms.

Behavioral Therapy

Behavioral therapy allows your child to identify and change negative behaviors. It can be done in an individual or group setting. It focuses more on one's behavior through their actions than their emotions. It also focuses on the development of self-control and self-esteem. It identifies your child's behavioral limits.

For a multimodal approach, both medication and behavior therapy are recommended, but for younger children (under age six), behavior management is encouraged before medicines are prescribed. The goal is to help your child bring positive changes to their behavior by changing their physical and social environments.

These behavior strategies can be learned and used at home and at school to succeed. It also helps in building social and interpersonal relationships. Parents and teachers must find a better way to communicate with your child and understand their needs. This also helps to enforce rules and discipline more effectively. The goal is to help your child be better in charge of their behavior. Consistency is key here.

How to Help Your Child

- Most adults do not understand the basic fact that every action has a consequence. This is because they never learned that value while growing up. Others who do learn it the hard way. Life has its ways to teach all of us what is of value. However, we cannot wait for life to be harsh on a child with ADHD. While we would like to protect these kids, it is equally important to prepare them as responsible adults to face the world. This can only be done through behavior, discipline, and values.

- Positive compliments help in building confidence in your child. These reinforcements in the form of rewards, words, privileges encourage good behavior. This helps your child differentiate between good and bad.

- Similarly, vocal opposition to negative behavior and withdrawal of rewards may discourage such action and words. This is a good technique to curate discipline in your child.

- The SMART plan that involves specific, measurable, achievable, realistic, time-bound goals and actions plays an important role here.
- A **tip for parents** would be to have a "point policy," where 3 points are awarded for a positive action and 3 points are deducted for a negative action. For example, if your child successfully completes a task, 3 points would be awarded, and if not, 3 points would be deducted. A task successfully done followed by a task not done would award them +3-3=0. With a score of zero out of six, your child learns that the negative fallout of their unfinished task will also affect the positive aspects of their life. All daily scores can be assessed by the end of the month. This is a great way to help children between the ages of 6 and 12 imbibe better habits.

Family Therapy

Medicines are not the ultimate remedies. Family support and parental guidance are necessary to boost your child's self-confidence and bring positive changes to their behavior. The effects of a pill could be fleeting and temporary, but the effects of family therapy are different. The traditional parenting methods are on the verge of disruption, and they do not work every time. This is where we need to reimagine our methods and expectations.

- Family therapy helps the household to run as a single unit.
- It gives space and significance to your child's place in the family and improves their emotional and social conduct.
- It helps ease some pressure off the parents' shoulders and makes it a shared responsibility rather than an individual burden.
- It gives a chance for new and effective methods of parenting.

Because therapies last longer without any side effects, younger kids must first be exposed to family therapy and then to medicines. Such conditioning also helps improve other mental health issues and related behavioral conditions. When family-focused, the therapy may:

- lessen the dosage of medicines
- improve relationships
- make the bonds stronger, especially parenting

- allow better monitoring
- lower stress levels
- make discipline more effective
- give rise to group brainstorming looking for common solutions
- encourage better conflict resolution
- sit well with the kid's personality, habits, and age since the family surrounds the child as the closest unit around them
- make the kid feel comfortable, safe, and secure

Even within the family, the top caregivers are the parents. A few quick tips for the parents would be the following:

- Draw limitations to your own labor. Do not overwork or overburden yourself with things that you cannot handle. Know your capacity well before you act.
- Set clear and proper guidelines with your child. You must know your child's expectations from you as much as you know about your expectations from your child.
- Have unfiltered conversations with the therapist about what you want changed and why. Understand the consequences well since

you would be touching your child's everyday life.

- Show patience, gratitude, and maturity. Do not be rude to your child in the process if they seem to fail you. They are doing it for the first time just as you.

- The sooner the integrated-parent child treatment begins, the better. It takes more than ten sessions to conquer all the new techniques for parenting. But one thing that you need to remember is that you are your child's first and foremost teacher and caregiver. No one else would understand your child's needs better than you.

- Get into a routine yourself to get your child into a routine. Do not be too disciplined or harsh on yourself, but a regular time frame around chores may help you manage your time and tasks better.

- Join a support group if you feel too tired. Similar stories, connections, and situations may encourage you to share information and ideas and better strategize to tackle this problem. You may also join an online group.

Group Therapy

Many times, children with ADHD are unaware of the impact their presence has on their surroundings. They are also not aware of the effects their hyperactivity, impulse control, restlessness, anxiety, and aggressiveness may have on other relationships. They may care for other people. They may not be acutely aware of the feelings of other people through intuition or perception.

When kids with ADHD are provided support and guidance from their peers in group sessions, these are called group therapy sessions. Interpersonal relationships, social skills, awareness, self-control, emotions, and behavior management are windows of opportunity acquired through skills and training. Kids, along with their peers, practice skills and strategies, to resolve conflict and anger, resolve problems, and control themselves to heighten awareness and lessen the impact of ADHD behavior on others.

WHAT TO KEEP IN MIND?

The training of primary caregivers is as important as that of children. This prepares the people around your child to react in a more considerate manner. The actions may be favorable or unfavorable, but the reactions determine how your child is perceived by parents and teachers. Hence, their behavior conditions and coaches your child.

Counseling sessions, training, and support groups allow the caregivers some time to understand themselves. These are immensely helpful because they help manage stress and emotions while teaching methods for positive parenting. Apart from this, the following areas can be kept in mind for building a practical and constructive relationship with a kid with ADHD:

- **Routine**: Maintaining a daily and timely routine is essential to your child's life because it teaches them the value of life. This is a great way to counter the notion that kids suffering with ADHD are slower than others. When kids manage their time better, they learn to save extra time. Timely waking up, taking baths, having meals, doing homework, and playing helps your child to have a healthy routine that activates both the body and mind. This also helps them to sleep better and on time.
- **Organization**: Organizing home and space is extremely important. Your child may have the need to place things in a sequence and order. They can also be taught to organize daily use articles to manage them better. Organizing

things according to sizes and colors also helps to reduce anxiety. They are also more likely to easily find these things whenever needed.

- **Focus**: Television, loud conversations, noises or music, computer games, screen time on the phone, and even a dimly lit room may distract your child to a great extent. Not just during homework, but even during mealtime or a fun activity like drawing or coloring, distractions must be kept away to help your child nourish focus and not channel energy into too many activities at once. These kids must also frequent heavily crowded places. Nature and natural settings and sounds are known to help kids retain focus.

- **Appreciation**: Hugs, compliments, treats, smiles, and favorite foods are quite the prizes that your little one's heart will cherish. These rewards and praises can encourage your child to make greater efforts in their next tries.

- **Options**: You may use the checklist, diagrams, and charts to keep your child engaged in the chore. The task can be made interesting by keeping the instructions brief and direct. The options at disposal must not be more than two. More options may distract your child. This exercise is necessary to improve their decision-making ability and choose a priority.

- **Realistic goals**: If, as a parent, you are getting impatient and are waiting for instant results, you would be highly disappointed. It takes big efforts and slow progress to make big and long-lasting positive impacts. Your child's goals must be reachable, realistic, and resounding. Your child's small steps toward learning must be their big window into experiencing the world of order and control. Because such discipline can be overwhelming, it is very important to turn one page at a time, because that is how you finish a big book.

- **Progress track**: Punishment is not the cure. Reward is. But the reward must not be the end. A progress track may help to keep a check of all the results that deserved a reward, and the ones that failed to reach the finish line. Children understand situations better than we think they do, and it is important to discuss their progress with them to give them a vision and motivate them toward hope. Plans must be flexible and re-evaluated whenever necessary.

- **Communication**: Coordinating your efforts with your child is very important. Similarly, coordinating them with your child's teacher or secondary caregiver is equally necessary. You all need to be on the same page if you have to read the same line. A good communication eases the task and earns your child's trust. Frequent friendliness is necessary in between spells of mild to strict monitoring. The therapist must also plan certain activities of your child with you the parent.

- **Peacefulness**: Not everyone has the choice of maintaining peace. However, when the reins are in their hands, parents must try to maintain decorum with warmth. Peace only prevails with love and affection. Some rules can be tightened only when some other ropes are loosened. Discipline must be exercised with calmness. Time slots can be made for productive work with breaks in between for fun, relaxation, and refreshment.

CONCLUSION

When we talk about ADHD, we need to first define help. Kids with ADHD need help from others to understand why they lack anything when compared with other kids. But here is the tricky part. The primary and secondary caregivers, mostly parents, teachers, nurses, and babysitters, need to make sure the child accepts that they are not short of any power that their peers have.

Being slow is not a hurdle. It must not be. Just as being anxious or confused must not be a hurdle. All kids face these issues to varying degrees. They all have different needs as well. Kids with ADHD have needs that must be understood by those surrounding them. A series of steps may help elevate self-awareness and involve education and positive, comforting communication that answers curious questions, all the while keeping the answers simple and concise.

The strategies must focus on unlocking the potential of the child. This is possible only with unconditional love and care. Love may provide the most important and crucial energy around a child to help them feel important. On the course to achieving the goal, some wars will be won, and others will be lost. Small steps toward the goal make all the difference. The goal should never be unrealistic expectations of perfection, but rather acceptance by the child that life will not be fair to them. The constant reminders about their strengths encourage the spirit of fortitude. This may help them feel good about themselves in a world that frowns on their (dis)abilities.

TAKE THE CHALLENGE AND STIMULATE THE BRAIN

Every child dealing with ADHD is different, and so are their challenges. The key to finding a fine balance is understanding the mind of your child. With this understanding, one needs to proceed toward cerebellar stimulation of your child. The cerebellum is located at the back and the base of the brain. It occupies 10% of the volume of the brain and contains 70–75% of its neurons. Its main function is to maintain coordination, balance, and physical movements, but it also has a central role in maintaining emotions and thoughts. It maintains an important connection with the frontal lobes, which play a decisive role in ADHD. The mind can also be made active in a few ways.

- One is by being physically and mentally active. While it is true that mental stimulation is very necessary to keep the brain active, physical exercise has a positive role in keeping the body and mind healthy and diminishing the extreme effects of ADHD in the life of a child. Physical exercises help stimulate the cerebellum. Ten to twelve minutes of physical movement, three times a day, will start showing results in three to six months. This shows noticeable improvements when your child manages their emotions, attention, physical functions and plans next actions. It is a powerful tool that activates the mind and brings more stability and patience. It releases good hormones and pumps more oxygen into the blood.
- Medication can work for some people. But at the same time, it may not work for many others. All the options must be considered before or with medication, but the option of medicine must not be ignored if others are not

working. This is because every ADHD challenge is different. Medication can be a game changer for some people when other efforts are falling short. A lot of times parents of kids with ADHD, shy away from this option to not make their child drug-dependent, but mind stimulators are not the villains here. Our faith should be in treatment and not fear.

- Education plays an important role in turning ADHD into one's strength. This education makes us more aware of the paradoxes that exist in the mind but also takes us deeper into the world of ideas and possibilities. It tells us that the mind is limitless, and through learning, talking, and investigations we may come face to face with the fascinating organ that is a lot more than just a wall of problems, symptoms, and signs. Education is the journey that allows learning better, owning the reality, mastering the techniques, and finally, earning the benefits.

- A creative outlet is more than a means of expression. It facilitates exploration of our true self and talents, and the need to engage the creative side of the brain to make it work. The more this creative journey is challenging, the more it matters to your child.

- Finally, a meaningful connection is the beginning of positive change. It is the supreme force that drives everything good in life. Connection to people and nature is vital to your child's life to inspire and be inspired. Disconnection affects people greatly. They may feel isolated and crestfallen, and social support, especially from family, may help your child bloom into a better version of themselves. Some people function and focus better in isolation. Their productivity may increase when they work alone, but survival is not possible without a genuine connection. Health, satisfaction, and longevity for a person with ADHD depend upon meaningful associations. Otherwise, this isolation can soon become the cause of anxiety, diseases, and disorders.

THE FIVE PS OF ADHD PROCESS REIMAGINED

People with ADHD, and everyone around them, must see this obstacle as a strength. Yes, it is a disadvantage to not be able to stay on a task when not interested. It can bore a person to death if there is no mental stimulation. But looking for challenges is the source of a *reju-*

venating and reimagined life. What is life without a challenge?

The first P in this important process has to be the **parents**. Parents are at the core of this re-imagination. They are the reason this book was written. We do not talk about parents much, and when we do, we hand them an instruction manual—not an easy and relatable read. Not to mention, a lot of parents are first timers with no previous child-rearing experience. Others who do still find it difficult to cope with their child because ADHD does not come with directives and mandates. Without the parents' help, the diagnosis and treatment of ADHD can never go in a positive and clear direction.

The second P is **positive**. The goal of this reimagination is to expand the positives and reduce the negatives. The pressure of ADHD can overwhelm a person, especially a child. This makes this condition unique. It is all about finding the right balance because ADHD has the power to pull down the positive energy of the child and parents in no time. Reactions and meltdowns can be unexpected and unpleasant. To counter these, one needs a practical dose of positivity now and then. This is true even for the parents and relatives of the ADHD child.

Professional experience is the third crucial aspect of this re-imagination. A professional who is experienced and trustworthy falls into this category. A pediatrician, psychologist, psychiatrist, neurologist, and the family's regular doctor are completely capable of diagnosing this condition. But the trick is to do background checks on these medical and mental health professionals because it is not necessary that those who think they understand ADHD will understand it well. There is a big difference between an accurate and complete diagnosis and guesswork and incomplete tests.

The fourth crucial P is the **power of purpose**. This alone shifts the gears of our reimagination process. It is the power that draws you in as a parent. We all understand diagnosis is necessary. But what next? What is the goal of this diagnosis? Simply depending on therapies and medicines will lessen the effects of ADHD temporarily. Understanding the causes and tapping a child's hidden potential must be the ultimate goal. Many parents are confused at this juncture. Where does one go for training and therapy? How do we cope with the struggle as a family? How do we nourish the child to be their most successful version? Parents would understand that this purpose is not found in isolation. This purpose is discovered when the family stands as a unit. The role of family and community is strategic in the life of every child, especially one with ADHD.

The last P is for **perfection,** or the illusion that we keep chasing. This deception snatches away our happiness and contentment. With the right combination of treatment (medication and therapy) and strategies, coping with this disorder is possible. But many parents either refuse to accept their child's condition or think that their efforts will "correct" the child's behavior.

The day we realize that perfection lies in the imperfections of beauty unique to every child, we will spare little kids and let them enjoy their childhood. It is not the disorder that induces anxiety and depression in a child and isolates them. It is the mindset of society and the pessimism with which we see anything that does not fit into our narrative of perfection. To the parents, I would say, "Please do not listen because there is no fault in your parenting. It is in your hands to decide the way your child will live their life. Minor changes, and your child will grow up to write another success story in the league of many. After all, it was the parents who were the unsung heroes of all these stories."

REFERENCES

Allen, S. (2020). *Our home can't withstand all of these emotional ADHD explosions!* ADDitude. https://www.additudemag.com/adhd-control-emotions-parent/

Anderson, D. (n.d.). *How to parent with ADHD: parenting skills and strategies.* ADDitude. https://www.additudemag.com/parenting-with-adhd-strategies/

Gilman, L. (2006). *How to succeed in business with ADHD?* ADDitude. https://www.additudemag.com/adhd-entrepreneur-stories-jetblue-kinkos-jupitermedia/

Hallowell, E. (2020). *Changing your perspective on ADHD.* Dr. Hallowell. https://drhallowell.com/2020/01/29/changing-your-perspective-on-adhd/

Hams, J. (2009, May 6). *ADHD – a parent's tale.* ABC Health & Wellbeing. https://www.abc.net.au/health/yourstories/stories/2009/05/06/2562327.htm

Institute, ADHD. (2019). *Impact of ADHD.* ADHD Institute. https://adhd-institute.com/burden-of-adhd/impact-of-adhd/

Jacobson, R. (n.d.). *School success kit for kids with ADHD.* Child Mind Institute. https://childmind.org/article/school-success-kit-for-kids-with-adhd/

Jaksa, P. (n.d.). *Mothering without smothering.* ADHD Center. https://www.addcenters.com/articles/mothering-without-smothering-how-to-avoid-being-an-overprotective-parent

Koplewicz, H.S. (n.d.). *Being an effective advocate of your child.* Child Mind Institute. https://childmind.org/article/being-an-effective-advocate-for-your-child/

Lavoie, R. (2018). *How to motivate (not demoralize) a student with ADHD.* ADDitude. https://www.additudemag.com/motivating-a-child-with-adhd-classroom-tips/

Low, K. (2018). *8 simple school strategies for students with ADHD.* Verywell

Mind. https://www.verywellmind.com/help-for-students-with-adhd-20538

Low, K. (2022). Why children with ADHD need structure and routines. Verywell Mind. https://www.verywellmind.com/why-is-structure-important-for-kids-with-adhd-20747

McQueen, J. (n.d.). *Family therapy for childhood ADHD: what to know.* WebMD. https://www.webmd.com/add-adhd/childhood-adhd/childhood-adhd-family-therapy

Miller, G. (2021). *ADHD parenting: 12 tips to tackle common challenges.* Psych Central. https://psychcentral.com/childhood-adhd/parenting-kids-with-adhd-tips-to-tackle-common-challenges

Nelson, W. (2006). *Why couldn't he be like any other boy?* ADDitude. https://www.additudemag.com/adhd-personal-stories/

Pagan, C. N. (n.d.). *Is your child ready to manage their ADHD medicine?* WebMD. https://www.webmd.com/add-adhd/childhood-adhd/self-care-adhd-children

Parekh, R. (2017). *What is ADHD?* American Psychiatric Association. https://www.psychiatry.org/patients-families/adhd/what-is-adhd#section_5

Poole, M. (2021, September 13). *How to Tackle ADHD and Home Organization Without the Stress.* Fast Brain. https://www.fastbraiin.com/blogs/blog/adhd-and-home-organization-without-the-stress

Pychyl, T. A. (2018, December 29). *ADHD and Academic Procrastination: A Success Story.* Psychology Today. https://www.psychologytoday.com/ca/blog/dont-delay/201812/adhd-and-academic-procrastination-success-story

Sederer, L. (2021, January 10). *ADHD 2.0 by Edward H Hallowell, MD and John J Ratey, MD.* Psychology Today. https://www.psychologytoday.com/us/blog/therapy-it-s-more-just-talk/202101/adhd-20-edward-h-hallowell-md-and-john-j-ratey-md

Sinfield, J. (2019). *7 secrets from a very successful ADHDer.* Untapped Balance. https://untappedbrilliance.com/7-secrets-from-a-very-successful-adhder/

Sosnoski, K. (2022). *3 ways to motivate a teen who has ADHD.* Psych

Central. https://psychcentral.com/adhd/motivational-strategies-for-children-with-adhd

Sreenivas, S. (n.d.). *ADHD and your child's self-esteem.* WebMD. https://www.webmd.com/add-adhd/features/adhd-and-child-self-esteem

Tiret, H., & Knurek, S. (2020). *Strategies to cope with family stress.* MSU Extension. https://www.canr.msu.edu/news/strategies_to_cope_with_family_stress

Wedge, M. (n.d.). *What we can learn from Michael Phelps about ADHD?* Psychology Today. https://www.psychologytoday.com/us/blog/suffer-the-children/201608/what-we-can-learn-michael-phelps-about-adhd

www.ingramcontent.com/pod-product-compliance
Lightning Source LLC
Chambersburg PA
CBHW020242130626
46549CB00005B/2025